A Voyage to Botany Bay

by

George Barrington

For More Books Please Visit the address below

http://www.barnesandnoble.com/s/WDS-Publishing

For Vintage Posters Please Visit

http://www.zazzle.com/oldposters

The once popular subject of this sketch was born about 1755, at a village called Maynooth, in Ireland; his father being a working silversmith, and his mother a mantua maker. Nearly ruined by law, they were unable to give their son an education suitable to the early abilities which he discovered. He was however taught to read and write; and a neighbouring surgeon instructed him in arithmetic, the elements of geography, and the general principles of grammar.

At sixteen, young Waldron was noticed and patronised by Dr. C--, a dignitary in the church of Ireland; and through whose influence he was placed at a free grammar-school in Dublin. But stabbing an older boy than himself with a penknife, from motives of revenge, he lost the support of his benevolent patron, and was severely chastised by the master. He could by no means forgive this degradation; and therefore resolved on leaving the school, and all his fair prospects behind.

His plan of escape was no sooner framed than it was carried into execution; but, previous to his departure, he found means to steal ten or twelve guineas from Mr. F--, the master of the school, and a gold repeating watch from Mrs. Gouldsborough, the master's sister. With this booty, a few shirts, and two or three pair of stockings, he silently, but safely, effected his retreat from the school-house, in the middle of a still night, in the month of May, 1771; and pursuing the great northern road all that night, and all the next day, he late in the evening arrived at the town of Drogheda, without interruption, without accident, and, in a great measure, without halting, without rest, and without food.

At Drogheda, Master Waldron connected himself to a company of strollers, and vagabondised about the country with indifferent success. The Theatrical Manager at length concerted a depredatory scheme with the young hero of his stage; and at intervals, they levied some heavy contributions. This great man, however, in the character of Waldron's servant, was detected in picking the pocket of the Right Hon. H--K--, and transported to America for seven years. His pupil shortly afterwards, attempting the property of Lord B---, at Carlow races, met the discipline of the course; and this disaster it was, that first determined him to select England as the theatre of his future exploits. He accordingly embarked on board the Dorset yacht, and arrived in England, in 1773, being then aged about eighteen.

In the metropolis he lived as Mr. Barrington, in a style of singular splendour, on the spoils which he had collected in Ireland; and by imposing on a gentleman, who had been passenger with him in the yacht, he gained his favour and confidence; finding by that means an introduction into the politest circles; from whence he extracted abundant plunder for a long time without being even suspected.

It would prove unuseful and even tasteless to follow Mr. Barrington through all his early scenes of dissipation and licentiousness: we shall therefore content ourselves with giving the most remarkable of his feats, as detached anecdote.

On forming a connection with one Lowe, which was but a short time previous to that evening of the month of January, which is observed as the anniversary of the Queen's birth-day, it was resolved on between them, that, habited as a clergyman, Mr. Barrington should repair to Court, and there endeavour, not only to pick the pockets of some of the company, but, what was a much bolder, and a much more novel attempt, to cut off the diamond orders of some of the Knights of the Garter, Bath, and Thistle, who, on such days, usually wear the collars of their respective orders over their coats. In this enterprize he succeeded beyond the most sanguine expectations that could have been formed, by either his new accomplice Lowe or himself; for he found means to take the diamond order of Lord C--, with which he got away from St. James's perfectly unsuspected.

This valuable acquisition, by the assistance and agency of Lowe, he disposed of for near eight hundred pounds to one Lursham, a Dutchman.

In the course of the winter of the year 1775, Prince Orlow, a Russian nobleman of the first rank and consequence, and high in the favour of his Sovereign, visited England. The splendour in which he lived, and the several circumstances of his story, and of his favour at the Court of Russia, were frequently noticed, and largely descanted on in the public prints; and particularly a gold snuff-box, set with brilliants, which was presented to him by the Empress, and which was generally valued at the enormous sum of thirty thousand pounds. This precious trinket excited, in an extraordinary manner, the attention of Barrington, and he determined to exert himself, in order to get it into his posession one way or other. For this a favourable opportunity presented itself one night at Covent-Garden playhouse; and this experienced pickpocket did not neglect to avail himself of it. He contrived to be near the Prince, and found means to convey the treasure, of which the acquisition was the great object of his avarice, or ambition, from his Excellency's waistcoat pocket, in which, according to the Russian custom, it was usually carried, into his own.

This operation was not, however, performed in such a manner as to escape instant detection: for the Prince felt the attack that was so impudently made upon him, and having reason to entertain some suspicion of Barrington, he immediately seized him by the collar. Such an action in a public theatre, naturally occasioned some bustle, as well as surprize; and during the confusion that ensued, he slipped the box into the nobleman's hand, who was, doubtless, glad to have recovered it with so much facility. The thief was, however, secured and committed to Tothill Fields Bridewell, for examination on the Wednesday following at Bow-street.

At the time appointed he was brought before Sir John Fielding, and examined, not only for the offence for which he was taken into custody, but also relative to his family, his profession, and his connections. On this occasion he represented himself as a native of Ireland, where his family, he said, were affluent and respectable; that he was educated in the medical line; and that he came to London to improve himself in the knowledge of it; all these circumstances he represented with becoming modesty, and with many tears, neither absolutely denying the crime with which he was charged at the playhouse, nor formally avowing his guilt. So that, after all, the Prince declining to proceed against him, and no prosecutor appearing, he was dismissed, after receiving a proper reprimand from the magistrate, and some seasonable admonition.

Partial to the theatre, he some time afterwards picked the pocket of Mr. Le Mesurier, at Drury-lane playhouse, for which offence he was instantly taken into custody. Charge of him was given to one Blandy, a constable, who, either through negligence or corruption, suffered him to make his escape. The proceedings against him were, however, carried on to an outlawry, and various methods were ineffectually taken for near two years to have him apprehended.

While the lawyers were outlawing him, and the constables endeavouring to take him, he was travelling in various disguises, and in various characters, through the northern counties of this kingdom. He visited the great towns in those parts, as a quack doctor, or as a clergyman. Sometimes he went with an E O table, and sometimes he pretended to be a rider to a manufacturing house at Birmingham or Manchester; and travelling on horseback, with a decent appearance and a grave deportment, the account which he thought proper to give of himself was credited without any difficulty, by those who thought proper to question him.

It, however, sometimes happened that he was known by gentlemen whom he met, particularly once in Lincolnshire, but no one offered to molest or interrupt him until he arrived at Newcastle upon Tyne, where on being recognised, he was suspected of picking pockets, and on enquiry he was found to be outlawed; on which he was removed by a writ of Habeas Corpus to London, and imprisoned in New-gate, where he arrived poor, emaciated, and dejected.

The companions of his life, as a distinguished character in his line, however, on learning his circumstances, made a subscription for him; by which they collected near an hundred guineas for his use; and by this seasonable supply he was enabled to employ counsel, and to take legal measures to have the out-lawry against him reversed.

This being done, he was tried for the original offence, that of stealing Mr. Le Mesurier's purse; and through the absence of the Rev. Mr. Adeane, a material witness for the prosecution, he was acquitted and discharged.

In 1777, previous to the transaction recited in the foregoing anecdote, Mr. Barrington was sentenced to the Woolwich Hulks, for stealing a watch, of little value, from a woman whose situation was more indigent than his own.

In this receptacle of wretchedness and vice, he found himself exposed to such complicated misery, as he had never before known, and to such fatal diseases as he had never before felt. He was fatigued with hard labour, and harrassed with all the evils of indigence, confinement and obloquy; yet he bore up against all the weight of woe under which he laboured, with a degree of patience, resignation, and constancy worthy of a better cause than that in which he suffered. Fortune, at length, declared in his favour, and freedom became the recompence of his exemplary conduct during the period of his captivity; for, on the recommendation of Messrs. Erskine and Duncan Campbell, the superintendants or governors of the convicts, a pardon was granted to him; and, after somewhat less than a twelve-month's severe sufferings on the Thames, he was set at large. However, in less than half a year after his enlargement from the Hulks, he was again detected by the vigilance of one Payné, at that time a very active peace-officer in the city, in the fact of picking pockets in St. Sepulchres church, during the time of the celebration of divine service, on a certain city festival; and having been convicted of this offence, on the clearest evidence, at the Old Bailey, he was a second time sentenced to hard labour on the Thames, and that for the term of five years.

Upon his trial on this occasion, it was that he appeared to have first distinguished himself as a public speaker. He endeavoured, with much art, but without any success, to work upon the feelings of the Court and Jury; but the proofs against him were so clear, that he was found guilty; and, pursuant to his sentence, he was removed once more to the Hulks at Woolwich, about the middle of the year 1778.

When he was this second time put on board one of these prison ships, he either found his sufferings more intolerable, or his situation to be more desperate, than they appeared to him on his first confinement; a circumstance which is said to have determined him upon suicide; and, in consequence of this impious resolution, he stabbed himself with a penknife. The wound, though deep and dangerous, did not prove mortal; and medical assistance being called in, and seasonably applied, a cure was effected. It was, however, effected very slowly; and the wound having been given in the breast, seemed in its effects, after near two years continuance, to bring a consumption on the unhappy patient.

While he remained in this deplorable situation, it happened, fortunately for him, that Sir M--L--, a gentleman of rank and consequence, happened to visit the hulks, and to enquire into the state of the convicts. This gentleman, who was of the most benevolent character, and possessed of the most feeling heart, was led by curiosity to converse with Barrington; and his emaciated and squalid appearance so moved him with compassion, that he applied for a remission of the remaining part of his sentence; which was granted on condition of his (Barrington) immediately leaving England on his enlargement, and never more returning to it; and in order to enable him to fulfil his promise, a sum of money was giving to him to defray the expence of his journey to Ireland, his native country.

Ireland proving too circumscribed for the display of his great abilities; and having narrowly escaped conviction before a Dublin Jury, Mr. Barrington resolved to visit his favourite London once more, however dangerous the attempt, and however awful the impending consequence. He put his design into execution; and after a few public essays at the Opera and the Theatres, he was taken up on suspicion; but nothing being proved against him, he was detained in Newgate at the instance of Mr. Duncan Cambell, for not fulfilling the terms of his liberation; and in that gloomy receptacle he served out the remainder part of his former sentence. With liberty, however, his aptitude toward pilfering returned; and he lived in a continual state of warfare and apprehension, till the event took place which led to an outlawry, as before related.

September 15, 1790, Mr. was arraigned at the Old Bailey bar, on an indictment, charging him with stealing, on the first of the same month, a gold watch, chain, and seals, and a metal key, belonging to Henry Hare Townsend, Esq. at Enfield, during the races held there. On the evidence, Mr. Barrington was found guilty; and sentenced to Botany Bay for seven years, where his good and prudent conduct has since procured him the office of Constable! and it is to be hoped, that his sound knowledge will induce him to hold that appointment long, very long, after the approaching expiration of his allotted servitude. Particulars Relating to the Trial and Conviction of George Barrington.

He was indicted for feloniously stealing on the first of September, at Enfield races, a gold watch, valued at forty shillings, and a seal also valued at forty shillings, the property of Henry Hare Townsend, Esq.

Mr. Townsend, the prosecutor, being first examined, deposed, that on the first of September, having entered a horse for the races at Enfield, he accordingly went there at one o'clock in the afternoon: he put his watch in his waistcoat pocket, as much for the convenience of looking at it, as to prevent the chain from soiling his breeches, which were of leather. About a quarter past two he felt his watch in his waistcoat pocket. As he was leading the horse, which was to run, up to the starting post, a person dressed in a light-coloured coat, rudely rushed in from behind him, and pushed against the arm which had hold of the horse; the same person again repeated his push, but in a more violent manner.

Mr. Townsend further deposed, that from the reiterated apparent insult offered him, he, accompanied with an oath, asked Barrington what he wanted? to which he returned no answer, but observed the prisoner looked much confused. The conduct on the part of Barrington appeared very odd; but he entertained no suspicion of having been robbed, until Mr. Blades came up to him, and asked him, if he had not been robbed? On feeling his pocket, he found his watch was gone. Mr. Blades informed him that Barrington was on the course, and he verily believed that he was the thief. After this they had agreed to say nothing about the matter, until they had found the supposed offender. They then walked about in search of Barrington, and at last saw him on the opposite side of the course; this was at the very moment when the horses were going to start, Nothing occurred till after the horses were past; after which they went up to him; and Mr. Townsend going behind him, seized him by the collar, and said--"You rascal, you have robbed me of my watch." No sooner had Mr. Townsend said the words, but he again laid hold of him fast by one hand and arm, and Mr. Blades took hold of the other, and conducted him to a booth.

Buxton Kendrick affirmed, that after he had been about a minute in the booth, he heard something rattle, and looking down, he saw the watch fall rather between his legs. John

Waldeck, Mr. Townsend's coachman, also declared, that he heard the watch jingle as it fell from the prisoner: that Barrington attempted to kick the watch further behind him; but that he picked it up, and gave it to Lady Lake, in the next booth, who was a relation of Mr. Townsend.

William Blades, the principal witness, deposed, that he saw Barrington at the races, he was near the stand, and close to Mr. Townsend; that he observed no conversation at the time passing between the prosecutor and prisoner. Soon after this he asked Mr. Townsend if he recollected a tall thin man, in a light-coloured coat, standing by him; which he said he did, but knew nothing of him. Blades after this informed Mr. Townsend, that he supposed he was robbed, which appearing to be the fact, they both went in search of the prisoner, whom they apprehended, as above related.

Mary Dandy deposed, that she was standing in the next booth, and saw the prisoner drop the watch out of his hand; after this, she looked him full in the face, and consequently could not tell whether he kicked it, or not. She at the same time accused him of throwing the watch down, but was immediately pulled back by some person near her.

Barrington made a long and specious defence, and among other things, charged the evidence with being imperfect, inconsistent, and, in some respects, unsafe, especially that of Mary Dandy.

Lord Chief Baron Eyre, having summed up the evidence in a clear and circumstantial manner, observed, that the prosecutor had demonstrated his lenity, by making the indictment only for single felony, when it might have been made capital.--The Jury, after a short deliberation, found the prisoner guilty.--Transportation for seven years.

The Chief Baron then addressed Barrington in a far different style from that he used before; his lordship observed, that he must consider himself as peculiarly fortunate in the lenity of his prosecutor: he said that he had had many warnings, not only from the fate of others, but the many narrow escapes he himself had had; and he regretted that talents like his should be employed in a manner so truly disgraceful to him: and (said his lordship), notwithstanding your life is now saved, I fear that these wicked habits are so far rooted in you, that your existence will terminate in a shameful spectacle.

Among other things said by Barrington in his address to the court, the following is not unworthy notice:

"The world has given me credit for much greater abilities than I am conscious of possessing: the world should also consider that the greatest abilities may be so obstructed by the ill-nature of some unfeeling minds, as to render them nearly useless to the possessor. And where was the generous and powerful man to come forward, and say--`Barrington, you have some abilities which may be of service to yourself and the public, but you have much obstruction--I feel for your situation, and shall place you in a condition to try the sincerity of your intentions; and as long as you act with diligence and integrity, you shall not want for countenance and relief?' Alas! my lord, had never the supreme felicity of having such comfort administered to his wounded spirits, as matters have unfortunately turned out." A Voyage to New South Wales.

Chapter I.

It was with unspeakable satisfaction that I received a summons to be ready early the next morning for my embarkation, agreeably to my sentence. I instantly made the most of my time, and by the assistance of a friend, procured a few pounds worth of necessaries for my voyage; government allowance being extremely slender, especially for one like me, who had hitherto been accustomed to most of the luxuries of the table. The news of my speedy departure brought several of my acquaintance to bid me adieu, and, with gratitude, I recollect that not one of them came empty handed; for, before the time of locking up. I had such a collection of ventures, that I doubted whether I should be permitted to take them all on board: had each of my shipmates been as well stocked, it would have needed a ship on purpose.

About a quarter before five a general muster took place; and having bid farewell to my fellow prisoners, we were escorted from the prison to Blackfriarsbridge by the city guard, where two lighters were waiting to receive us. This procession, though early, and but few spectators, made a deep impression on my mind; and the ignominy of being thus mingled with felons of all descriptions, many scarce a degree above the brute creation, intoxicated with liquor, and shocking the ears of those they passed with blasphemy, oaths, and songs, the most offensive to modesty, inflicted a punishment more severe than the sentence of my country, and fully avenged that society I had so much wronged.

Absorbed in the most humiliating meditation, the objects we passed going down the river were totally unnoticed by me; nor was I rouzed from my lethargy till I received a violent blow on the head, which I took at first for a stroke with a stick, but on looking around me found we were alongside the ship, and that the injury I had sustained proceeded from the boatswain, who, standing on the gangway, had thrown a small coil of rope for some one on board the lighter to take hold of, to bring us alongside, and which unluckily came in contact with my head; this circumstance occasioned a laugh at my expence; but as I have always found that chagrin and ill-humour encreases the mortification, I stifled my real sensations, and seemed to join the mirth. In my turn I ascended the ship's side, and to my great satisfaction, the first person I cast my eyes on was my particular friend, whose generous exertions not only procured me stowage for my packages, but also the liberty of walking the deck, unencumbered by those ignominious and galling chains, which my past conduct had consigned me to. Not content with these services, he prevailed on the boatswain to admit me into his mess, which was composed of the second mate, carpenter and gunner, who cheerfully acquiesced, on receiving my proportion towards defraying the extra requisites for the mess during the voyage. My benefactor having rendered my situation thus comfortable, bade me farewell, and left me: my heart swelling with gratitude, was too full, and interdicted all verbal acknowledgements; but the remembrance is too strongly engraven thereon for the most distant time to effect the slightest cradication.

My fellow prisoners, to the amount of upwards of two hundred, were all ordered into the hold, which was rendered as convenient as circumstances would admit, battens being fixed fore and aft for hammocks, which were hung seventeen inches apart from each other; but being encumbered with their irons, together with the want of fresh air, soon rendered their situation truly deplorable. To alleviate their condition as much as was consistent with the safety of the ship, they were permitted to walk the deck in turn, ten at a time: the women, of whom we had six, had a snug birth made for them, and were kept by themselves.

My messmate, the boatswain, had provided me with a neat snug hammock, and gave me a birth next his own; at the same time addressing some of his shipmates who were present, with "Lookee, my hearts, as I know you are all above distressing a gentleman under misfortunes, I'm sure you will consent to his having this here birth; but if so be as how any of you don't like it, why you may have mine--It isn't the first time I have prick'd for the softest plank." Whether from the oratory of my new friend, or the insinuating appearance of a large cann of flip, produced from an ample liquor-case, which promised a succession of the same arguments, the iron muscles of his auditors were softened down to a significant smile, and universal nod of assent. The settling of this important business afforded me great satisfaction, as it not only assured me a comfortable birth for my hammock, but a place also for my little property, which I could have immediately under my eye.

We lay about a week at Long Reach when we dropt down to Gravesend; here the captain came on board, and some soldiers of the New South Wales corps; we got under weigh the next morning, and proceeded to the Downs; it blowing strong to the westward, we came to an anchor. The wind veering about, at day-break we were again under sail, and arrived at the Mother-Bank, where lay several other transports for the same destination.

It was about ten days before we were ready to sail from hence, the interval being employed in getting fresh stock, and replenishing our water. On the report of our being ready for sea being made to the admiral, a lieutenant of the navy came on board, as agent for transports, and immediately made the signal for the masters of the other ships to come on board, to whom he delivered their sailing instructions; and on the following morning made the signal to weigh: by a quarter past nine we were under an easy sail; and it blowing a stiff easterly breeze, we ran through the Needles: it was delightful weather, and the prospect on each hand must have afforded the most agreeable sensations to every beholder, and is, perhaps, as rich and luxuriant as is any where to be met with; but, alas! it only brought a fresh pang to the bosom of one who in all probability was bidding it adieu for ever.

The weather continuing moderate, and the wind fair, we imperceptibly glided down the channel, and had lost sight of Old England before I turned out the next morning. My frequent trips from Ireland to England had, in some measure, inured me to salt water, nor did I want my sea--legs in a most violent gale, which took place the third day after we lost sight of the land, and which for near ten hours baffled the skill of all hands: two men were blown from the main-top-sail yard, and the sail split to ribbons; all our endeavours to save the men proved ineffectual. Soon after our fore top-mast went over the side, and carried four men and two boys with it; but they were providentially taken up, having kept fast to the wreck. By the indefatigable exertions of the seamen, the remainder of the sails were handed, and the ship greatly eased, carrying only a storm stay-sail; the sea running very high and irregular, rendered it very uncomfortable; and not being capable of any service upon deck, I retired to my hammock, where I buried all thoughts of the contentious ocean in a sound sleep, from which I was awaked by the shrill whistle of my messmate, piping all hands to breakfast; the cheering sound of "steady" from the helmsman saluting mine cars, and the quietness of the ship assured me the gale was past. Having huddled on my cloaths, I found, on my ascending the deck, the storm had subsided, the wind perfectly fair, and the ship jogging on under an easy sail, at the rate of about seven miles an hour.

Chapter II.

This danger was succeeded by one that had nearly proved much more fatal; the captain, with great humanity, had released many of the convicts who had been in a weakly state, from their irons; and as I have before observed, they were allowed alternately, ten at a time, to walk the deck. Two of them, Americans, who had some knowledge of navigation, prevailed upon the majority of their comrades to attempt seizing the ship, impressing them with the idea that it would be easily effected, and that they would carry her to America, where every man would not only attain his liberty, but receive a tract of land from Congress, besides a share of the money arising from the sale of the ship and cargo.

These arguments had the desired effect, and it was determined determined the first opportunity that a part of those on the deck should, while the officers were at dinner, force the arm-chest, which was kept on the quarter-deck, at the same time make a signal to two of them, who should be keeping the centinels in discourse, to attack them, get possession of their arms, and pass the word for those below to rush upon deck.

This conspiracy was conducted with the greatest secrecy, and put in execution with equal spirit and audacity. A favorable opportunity presenting itself, the captain and most of the officers being below, examining the stowage of some wine, a cask having leaked out in the spirit room, I was the only person on the deck excepting the man at the helm, hearing a scuffle on the main deck. I was going forward, but was stopped by one of the Americans, followed by another convict, who made a stroke at me with a sword he had wrested from one of the centinels, which was put aside by a pistol which the other had just snapped at me; I snatched up a handspike luckily in my reach, and brought the foremost to the ground; the man at the helm had quitted the wheel, and called up the captain. I still kept my situation, guarding the passage of the quarter-deck, my antagonists having retreated a few paces, but being joined by many others, were rushing on me, when the discharge of a blunderbuss from behind me among them wounding several, they retreated, and I was immediately joined by the captain and the rest of the officers, who, in a few minutes, drove them all into the hold. An attempt of this kind required the most exemplary punishment; accordingly two of the ringleaders were instantly hung at the yard-arm, and several others severely flogged at the gangway.

As soon as the conspirators were re-ironed, and the tranquility of the ship restored, the captain paid me many handsome compliments, in having, as he was pleased to say, saved the ship, and assured me that when we arrived at the Cape, he should, on the part of his owners, think it his duty to reward the service, I had by my courage and presence of mind rendered them; at the same time he gave his steward orders to supply me with any thing I might have occasion for from his store-room during the voyage.

I soon experienced the good effects of my late behaviour, as seldom a day passed but some fresh meat or poultry was sent me by the captain, which considerably raised me in the estimation of my messmates, who were no ways displeased at the substitution of a sea pie made of fowl or fresh meat, to a dish of lobscouse, or a piece of salt junk.

With a settled north-westerly breeze we gradually proceeded to the southward, at the rate of between eighty and one hundred miles in twenty four hours: we soon reached the island of Teneriffe, and came to an anchor in the bay of Santa Cruz, which is defended by several batteries of three or four guns each, at certain distances from each other, round the bay, and close to the water's edge; their principal fort is near to the landing place, and mounts a number of heavy cannon: it is a strong work, but there being a good depth of water close in shore, it could not sustain the attack of two ships of the line, though the whole of the batteries mount more than one hundred pieces of cannon.

The town of Santa Cruz is very irregularly built, the principal street being so broad, that it looks more like a square than a street; the house of the governor, which is at the upper end, is a very indifferent looking building, and has more the appearance of an auberge than the palace of a Spanish grandee; at the other end is a square monument, commemorating the appearance of our Lady to the Guanches, the Aborigines of the island. The outskirts appear like a deserted village rather than a place of trade, many of the houses being either half built, or fallen to decay from some cause or other; and the stone walls, which were their principal fences, are broken down and in ruins.

Some of the officers having obtained leave from the agent of transports to visit the town of Oratava, a few miles from Santa Cruz, we having completed our water and fresh stock, and waiting for the other transports who had not been so alert; on my expressing a desire to see the town, I was permitted to be of the party. The country is exceedingly beautiful and fertile, notwithstanding the frequent convulsions of the neighbouring volcanos: we arrived at Oratava about noon, and by signs, for none of us were masters of the language, we got a few eggs, and plenty of small wine. We had scarcely taken our seats, when we were relieved from the inconvenience attending our not being acquainted with the language, by the arrival of an old Spanish soldier, who had been some time a prisoner in England, and spoke our tongue tolerably well: we informed him we had come from Santa Cruz to take a nearer view of the Peak, and, if time would admit, to ascend it. He said it was impossible at this time of the year, as no guides would undertake to accompany us, and that several of the goatherds who had ventured after their goats, had perished from the intenseness of the cold, but that he would take us as far as was prudent for us to venture. We thanked him for the offer, and accordingly walked out a league from the town into the plain, which extends to the base of the Peak, and had a full view of this stupendous mountain. Immense quantities of lava, and huge fragments of rocks evidently vomited from the crater of the volcano, covered the plains, and nearly reached the town: we gathered some small pieces which had been sparred off, and found them impregnated with inflammable matter, and as hard as flint. I measured one of the pieces of rock with some twine I had about me, and afterwards found it was near seventy feet in circumference. Our time being short, and the weather intensely cold, we returned to Oratava, and got some salt fish, with a few hard eggs for supper, to which our old soldier invited himself, but amply repaid us for his intrusion by a lively and humorous description of the squabbles of his neighbours, the knavery practiced by the mountaineers on the curious and exploring stranger; his own heroism against the Moors, and at the siege of Gibraltar, where he was taken prisoner; with his amours while in England: the intervals were supplied by several songs from a company of muleteers, who by their extreme vociferation entirely discomposed the serenity of our loquacious guest, and, but for my mediation, would have produced a serious quarrel between them. Our leave of absence from the ship extending till sunset the following day, we enquired of our interpreter if we could be provided with beds; he gave us to understand that a bed was an article of luxury little known to the generality of the Oratavians, but he would get us mats to sleep on, which we were fain to be contented with; and in spite of the indefatigable labour of myriads of every species of vermin, I enjoyed as pronound a sleep, as though I had rested on a bed of down. A little before sunrise we were waked by the veteran, who had come to partake of our breakfast and shew us the town. Not having stripped, we soon made our appearance at the table, where he had provided half a dozen small loaves, some baccalo, and a quantity of dried grapes; he had also boiled a large iron kettle of coffee, but there being no sugar or milk at hand, we were glad to substitute some flasks of Teneriffe for our beverage.

Oratava is situated on the declivity of a rugged hill, gradually sloping to the sea, and commands a fine view of the bay, which, from the number of shoals, will only admit ships of a small draught of water, and here merchantmen of this description generally anchor, as wine, fruits, and vegetables, are procured at Oratava much cheaper than at Santa Cruz. It is certainly the most fertile side of the island, and, in a great measure, supplies all the rest. Nothing can be more charming or romantically situated than this delightful spot: the houses are low, but remarkably neat, and of white stone. On one side the street runs a pleasant rivulet from a copious spring of the clearest and sweetest water, which, in its progress over a rugged pavement, murmurs most agreeably along. Hills rising above hills, crowned with woods of the most luxuriant foliage, and beautifully canopied with varicgated clouds; and the stupendous Peak towering its majestic head above the whole, forms a prospect most sublimely interesting.

The surrounding vallies, adorned with vineyards, and watered by innumerable streams, forming naturally cascades, complete the picture.

At noon we began to think of returning to the ship; and taking leave of Don Gasparo, the old soldier, we reached Santa Cruz by sunset, and one of the boats being luckily on shore, immediately went on board, highly gratified with our excursion.

Chapter III.

THE ships having completed their watering, the signal was made for every person belonging to the fleet to repair on board their respective vessels, and the next morning the signal to get under weigh: with a pleasant breeze, we soon lost sight of the land. We steered to the south--west till we were in the meridian of St. Jago, when we shaped our course with an intention of coming to an anchor in Port-au-Praya bay; but when we opened the bay were taken aback, and a stiff breeze blowing direct in our teeth, it was thought that an attempt to gain the bay would be attended with some risk and much loss of time; it was therefore determined to give up the idea, and a signal was made for that purpose, we then shaped our course to the southward, and as we crossed the equinoctial line, the ceremony of shaving and ducking was punctually observed: at noon a hoarse voise hailed the ship, as from the sea, with "Ho! the ship, ho!" which was answered by one stationed for the purpose, with "Hallo! what ship's that?" "The Albemarle." "I don't recollect her passing this way before--I shall come on board and examine her." Upon which half a dozen most grotesque figures entered the ship, as if from the bosom of the deep; having previously slung a grating under each bow as a stage to ascend from: with great solemnity they proceeded to the quarter-deck: the principal personages were Neptune and Amphitrite, attended by their nymphs and neriads, personated by the oldest seaman in the ship, but so disfigured with red ochre, robes, and wigs made of ravelled spun yarn, that it was a difficult matter to recognize their persons. After receiving a double toll from the captain, it being the first time of the ship's crossing the line, consisting of half a gallon of liquor, and two pounds of sugar, they in turn questioned every person on deck. When any one said he had crossed before, and had not, his watery majesty, with great dignity, turning to one of his attendants, who held a large book, said, "Look if you have this gentleman down in my log-book?" which being answered in the negative, the rum and sugar was instantly demanded. When it came to my turn, my friend, the captain, desired them to put my quota down to him. Having finished with the quarter-deck, they proceeded to the examination of their own comrades, after having prepared for the ceremony of treating those who would not pay with a view of Neptune's cellar; for this purpose they made a tackle fast to the mainyard-arm, through which they rove a rope, with an iron crow made fast to the end for a seat. The only exhibition was on the person of the cook, who not being of the most conciliatory disposition, most of the ship's company owed him a grudge; and as he peremptorily refused to pay, although in his power, they placed him on the crow, and brought the yard-rope between his legs, making another fast round him, to prevent a possibility of his falling; they then swung him off, and running him close up to the yard, soused the poor devil from the height of near fifty feet into the water; this they performed thrice: when they took him on board he was so much exhausted that his life was thought in danger, which put an end to this part of the ceremony, and the other defaulters were let off with only a shaving, performed by Neptune and his assistants: the party was seated on a piece of board placed across a large tub; the razor part of an iron hoop, and the soap not the finest Windsor, but a composition of tar, tallow, and every filth they could collect: the disagreeableness of this operation, exclusive of the smart, the hand of the shaver not being of the lightest, occasions a struggle to get from under it, in which the board whereon he is seated gives way, and poor pilgarlick is unexpectedly emerged over head and ears in bilge water. Those destined for this operation are kept close prisoners, so that they are totally ignorant of what they are to go through, but when the ordeal is once passed, they think no more of it, but shake their ears, and assist on carrying on the joke. The forfeits made them all as merry as grigs, and the day closed with dancing and songs on the forecastle, and every body (the cook excepted) forgot their temporary mortifications, and joined in the evening's conviviality.

A most favourable breeze wafted us pleasantly along till we made Cape Frio: at midnight we were abreast of the cape, which is a small island, distant two or three miles from the main land. We had very little wind and variable weather between the Cape and Rio Janeiro, a distance of fifty or sixty miles. A spurt of wind from the sea carried us within the islands, when we came to an anchor off the harbour's mouth. The next morning the agent went on shore to wait on the victory, and in the afternoon we weighed and sailed into the harbour; as we passed the fort we saluted them with thirteen guns, which was returned by eleven (we not being a man of war) and came to an anchor abreast the town. The ships in general were remarkably healthy, and had hitherto buried but few of the convicts; in our passage from Teneriffe to this place we lost only four men and one woman, which is a very inconsiderable number, considering their confined state, change of climate, and unwholesomeness of living so long entirely on salt provisions. Fresh meat and vegetables were brought from the shore immediately on our coming to an anchor, and several country boats, with pines, bananas, oranges, and every species of tropical fruits, came alongside, of which the convicts had a certain proportion served them; the fruits being in such plenty, that the expence of distributing a few to each individual every morning was very inconsiderable.

The harbour is very commodions, and will contain almost any number of ships, where they may ride in perfect security from bad weather. The city of St. Sebastian is tolerably large, and regularly built; but from its being situated on low swampy ground, surrounded by high hills, it is entirely excluded from the refreshing sea and land breezes, so that in the summer months it is insupportably hot, and of course very unhealthy. Some few of the streets are pretty wide, but in general, they are rather too narrow; the square opposite the landing-place is spacious, and on the south side stands the palace of the viccroy, a very handsome stone building, and is said to be very richly ornamented within. The inside of the churches are decorated with the utmost profusion, and most of them furnished with an excellent organ, and tolerable good pictures over the different altars.

Here mechanics and tradesmen carry on their business in distinct parts of the town, particular streets being appropriated for particular trades: here you will find a whole street of gunsmiths, another of taylors, a third of carpenters, &c. &c.

The numerous forts and batteries which surround St. Sebastian give it an air of strength; but an enemy getting possession of the island of Cobres, which is very near to and overlooks the town, assisted by a few large ships, for which there is plenty of water, would soon oblige it to capitulate.

The produce and exports of Rio Janeiro are gold, sugar, rice, coffee, and most of the valuable drugs: we took a collection of seeds, and some young shoots of the tamarind, banana, orange, lemon, and guava trees, in order to try them on the soil of New South Wales.

Chapter IV.

WE lay here about three weeks, when the sick being pretty well recovered, the ships replenished with water, and loaded with vegetables and fruits of all kinds, the signal was made for sailing, and for the first three or four days we proceeded with a brisk north-easterly wind, when suddenly it became dark and cloudy, with tremendous peals of thunder and vivid flashes of lightning from every part of the horizon, attended with violent squalls of wind, but of no long continuance. At day-break the wind shifted to the south ward, and we had a series of fine weather till we arrived at the Cape of Good Hope, on the twentieth of July, and about sunset came to an anchor in Table Bay.

This being the last port we could touch at for refreshments during the remainder of the voyage, all hands set to work to procure such articles as they might stand in need of, as well for their present consumption, as for their future comfort in the new colony.

Early in the morning the captain ordered the pinnace to be manned, and went on shore; from whence he returned about noon, and sending for me aft, gave me an order on a merchant in Cape Town for one hundred dollars; at the same time telling me that I might at any time take the opportunity of the boats going on shore, to visit the town as often as I pleased, only speaking to the officer on deck when I was so disposed. The confidence he reposed in me struck me more forcibly than the money, and I was really so confused that I could scarcely articulate my acknowledgements.

During our stay here I visited the town almost every day, taking care to be on board by sunset; and laid out the money I had received in such articles as were most in request in New Holland.

On entering a house in Cape Town, you are always presented with a Sopi, that is to say, a glass of arrack, geneva, or perhaps French brandy; geneva, however, is the common morning dram. Before they sit down to table, the etiquette is to offer a Sopi of white wine, in which alloes or wormwood have been steeped, to create an appetite; at table they drink wine and beer indiscriminately. The beer is much esteemed, but they place a higher value on English porter. After the desert, which is always plentifully supplied, they bring pipes and tobacco, and continue drinking and smoking till late in the evening. This is their usual manner of living, with the exception of those in indifferent circumstances, who drink their own wine; but in this particular the vanity of the inhabitants is often highly ridiculous: one day as I was walking with an acquaintance I had made at the Cape, he made me observe a man seated at the door of his house, who seeing we were near him, began calling to his slave to bring him some red wine, though he assured me he had not a single drop in his house, and that most likely he had not tasted wine ten times in his life. When we had passed a little way, I turned and saw that his slave had brought him a glass of beer, which he with great ostentation deliberately drank off. For twelve miles round the Cape the colonists do not employ the Hottentots, chusing rather to purchase negroes who are more industrious and trust-worthy. The Hottentot, careless and inconstant by nature, often go away from their master on the prospect of hard work, and frequently leave them in embarrassment; the negroes desert also, but vain are their efforts to regain their liberty; they are soon retaken and sent to the bailiff of the canton, from whom they are redeemed by the proprietor for a small sum. Their correction is much less severe than one would expect: indeed there are few places where slaves are treated with more humanity than at the Cape.

The Creole slaves are most esteemed at the Cape, and fetch double the price of any other; if they are initiated in any business, their price is exhorbitant. A good cook is worth from eight to twelve hundred rix--dollars: mechanics double that sum; and others in proportion. They are commonly neatly dressed but walk barefooted, as a mark of slavery. There are none of that insolent tribe called footmen; luxury and pride not having yet introduced that useless lumber in the antichambers of the opulent.

The negroes of Madagascar and Mosambique are looked upon as the most ingenious and best workmen; they are also the most affectionate and faithful to their masters; when they are first landed at the Cape, they usually sell for one hundred and twenty to one hundred and fifty piastres a head. The Indians are more employed in household work in the town; there also some Malayans, but they are the most subtile and dangerous of all other slaves, frequently assassinating their masters or mistresses. When taken, they go to execution with the greatest indifference. I heard one of these wretches publicly declare, at the place of execution, that he was glad he had committed the crime, as they were only going to send him to his native country: it is a matter of wonder with me, that these ideas are not productive of much greater mischiefs.

I frequently dined at a Table d'Hote, or ordinary, where I fell in with a very intelligent Frenchman, who had traversed great part of the interior of the country, and from time to time related many entertaining particulars; from among which I selected the following account of one of his journies to the country of the Auteniquas, which I hope will not appear tedious to my readers.

"A traveller having arrived at the Cape, and signifying his intention of visiting the interior of the country, I immediately offered him my services. The bargain was soon struck, and I instantly set about procuring the necessary articles for the journey. We set out on our expedition in the middle of December, when I led the way towards Dutch

Hottentote, our company consisting of four horses, two of which were mounted by my master and myself, the others by two Hottentots, in case any accident should befall ours; there were three other natives, and each his dog: we stopped at the decline of day at the foot of those high mountains that border the east of the Cape.

"After two days journey we passed a little rivulet, and arrived at a wood called Le Bois de Grand Pere, near the country of the Auteniquas, which we found inhabited from the summit of the mountains to the water's edge by the colonists, who breed vast quantities of cattle, make butter, gather honey, cut wood for fuel, as well as for the mechanic; these articles are all sent to the Cape. It is astonishing that these people who have such plenty of timber, do not build themselves tenable houses, instead of being content with miserable huts, formed of hurdles covered with earth. The skin of a buffalo, stretched on four stakes, serves for a bed; a mat closes the door-way, which is also the window; two or three clumsy stools, some pieces of plank joined together make their table, and an ill-made box, of about two feet square, compose the whole furniture of one of these dens. In other respects these people live luxuriously; they have plenty of game and fish, and enjoy the advantage over the other colonists, in having all the year without interruption their gardens well stocked with all kinds of vegetables.

"These advantages are owing to the goodness of the soil, and the natural waterings from the various rivulets that wind and cross each other in a thousand different directions, laying under contribution, if it may be so expressed the four seasons of the year.

"In searching for a touraco, which Monsieur my master had shot, he fell into a pit upwards of twelve feet deep, which had been dug by the Hottentots, to entrap wild beasts, particularly the elephant. Fortunately the hole was empty, and he had the good fortune to escape being impaled alive on the pointed stakes fixed at the bottom of these pits: they are generally slightly covered over with slender branches of trees, and the interstices filled with turf and moss; the roots most anxiously sought after by the elephant are strewed on the surface, and the unwieldly animal eagerly pressing forward after his favourite food, is easily entrapped by the wily Hottentot into the snare: being wounded by the fall he is soon dispatched.

"After many fruitless efforts to extricate himself, I being at some distance with the Hottentots, he fired his fusee, and by that means brought us back to his assistance. This accident, however serious, did not prevent him pursuing the wounded bird, which at length he found, and considered the acquisition as a full compensation for all his perils. The touraco is as agreeable in its form, as in the sweetness and melody of its notes; it is of a bright green, a turf of the same colour, bordered with white, adorns its head; its eyes a sparkling red, with a streak over them of the most dazzling white; its wings are a beautiful purple, waving to the violet, according to the point of light in which it is viewed. It is reckoned by the naturalists a species of the cuckoo; but they have been much mistaken, as it has not the least affinity with that bird. The cuckoo, in every part of the world, subsists on snails and insects, but the touraco is fruvigorous. In whatever part of the world the cuckoo may be, it is remarkable that she never builds a nest, but lays her eggs in those of other birds, and by this means saves herself the trouble of rearing her young; the touraco on the contrary, is careful of its family, builds a nest, and hatches her own eggs; this difference in their disposition is, I think, a sufficient reason to prove them a particular species."

Chapter V.

"WE had scarce recovered from this accident when one of the Hottentots came running up to me, and said he had discovered the haunt of an elephant. After some hours fatigue, painfully tracing him through a thick part of the wood, rendered almost impassable from the thorns and briars, we arrived at an open part of the forest, in which was a clump of shrubs and under wood: here we stopped while one of the Hottentots ascended a tree; after looking round him, he clapped his finger on his mouth as a token for us to be silent, then by opening and closing his hand several times (a sign before agreed upon) gave us to understand how many elephants he had discovered.

"We now held a council of war, the result of which was, that the person who had seen them from the tree should lead us as near as possible through the bushes to the spot where he had discovered them. In a few minutes I was very near one of those enormous animals, which I did not immediately perceive, not that fear had fascinated my sight, but that I could scarce believe that the prodigious immoveable mass beneath me was the animal we had so much wished to encounter. It should be observed we were on a hillock which raised us above the back of the animal; I still kept looking farther on, and rather took what was so near me for a fragment of rock than a living creature. The Hottentot now cried out, 'See, see there! there he is,' with a tone of the utmost impatience. At length a slight motion caught my eye, and immediately after the head and tusks, which the enormous body had in part concealed, were turned towards me; Monsieur, who was close behind me, without losing time, let fly at him; I immediately followed his example, and both shots took place in his head; he stag gered and fell: the noise frighted the rest, and they to near the number of thirty, scampered off as fast as their unweildy corporations would permit them. This was but the prelude to a more animated scene.

"While we were examining the animal we had killed another passed just by us, which was fired at by one of the Hottentots, and by the blood that trickled down his huge shoulders I imagined he was mortally wounded, and immediately pursued him. He would have laid down, but was prevented by our repeated firing; he then took to the thickest part of the wood; we followed him into a thicket, in which was a number of decayed trees, that had fallen through age. The beast now became enraged from the number of his wounds, and made furiously at a Hottentot who had just discharged his piece at him, and at an instant trod him to death, and thrusting one of his tusks into the body, with a toss threw it upwards of thirty yards from him. We were about five and twenty paces from the poor fellow, my master a few paces behind me. I was too much encumbered for speed, my carbine being very heavy, and having a good deal of ammunition, together with a net containing several large birds, slung across my shoulder: I ran with all my might, but the enraged animal no sooner cast his angry eyes on me, than he pursued me at a full gallop, and gained ground every instant. More dead than alive through fear, abandoned by the Hottentots, who checked by the fate of their comrade, were less courageous than usual, the only chance I had was to lie down close to the trunk of a large tree that was near me, which I had scarce time to accomplish before the animal ran over it; but scared at the hooting of the Hottentots instantly stopped as it were to listen. I could easily have hit him from my situation had I chose, but although my piece was loaded, I restrained firing; for though he had received so many wounds I despaired to disable him by a single shot, so kept my situation, every moment expecting to become a prey to the enraged beast.

"The Hottentots having lost sight of me, as I lay close under the tree, not daring to stir, and not answering to their repeated cries, were persuaded. I was already crushed to pieces, made the woods re-echo with their shouts. The elephant turning hastily round, passed me a second time, and stepping over the tree not six yards from, went off on a full gallop. I sprung on my feet as soon as he had passed, and, showing myself to my companions, fired another shot after him, which did not stop his career, but rushing into the thickest part of the woods, disappeared.

"The report of my piece was an universal signal of joy. I was immediately surrounded by the Hottentots, whose countenances beamed the most lively and disinterested emotions of gladness: my master in the most affectionate terms expressed his satisfaction at my escape, pressing me eagerly in his arms. Night drawing on, we returned to find the elephant we had killed in the morning. The carcase was already in the possession of several large birds of prey, who had lost no time, having already made great progress in its dissection.

"Fires were now quickly kindled; and our attendants, after having pitched the tent, began to shew their skill in cooking. They cut off several steaks to broil for themselves, dressing a part of the trunk for us: it was the first time I had ever tasted this kind of food, but I determined it should not be the last, as I thought it delicious. Having settled the necessary preliminaries of watching round the tent, we went to rest, with as much composure as though we were at an inn; nor were we disturbed till sunrise, when we set forward on our journey. As we passed a small river we met a company of Hottentots, of about a score, who had fled from the wars of the Caffres. By our guides we learnt that those people are most vilely calumniated: the perpetual vexations and tyrranny of the colonists gave rise to those wars, in which the Caffres have been represented as ferocious animals, nurtured with human gore, sparing neither age nor sex, and totally regardless of the rights of hospitality. The colonists often form pretences of losing their cattle, purposely to make inroads into the Caffre settlements, exterminating whole hordes without distinction of age or sex, carrying away their herds, and laying waste the country; this being an easier method of obtaining cattle than rearing them.

"In destroying a small settlement of Caffres, a child of about twelve years of age escaped the general carnage, by concealing himself in a hollow tree, but, unfortunately, was discovered by one of the marauders, who determined to make a slave of his prize. The commander of this barbarous detachment peremptorily laid claim to the little trembling prisoner; the captor as firmly refused to deliver him up, which so enraged the savage leader that he ran with the utmost fury at the innocent object of the dispute, exclaiming 'If I must not have him, neither shalt thou!' and accompanied these words with a blow of his sabre, which laid the unfortunate victim dead at his feet.

"About noon one of our people, who had gone on some hundred yards before us, came running back with evident marks of confusion: on enquiring the cause, he told us there was a lion couching in a thicket a little a head of us, and that he would certainly attack us, if we proceeded. We immediately halted to consult what was to be done: Monsieur, desirous of adding the spoil of the king of the forests to his other acquisitions, decided on the attack. Accordingly the horses and dogs were given in charge to one of the natives to keep them back, and we, to the number of five, marched on, keeping a sharp look out. We had proceeded near half a mile, and finding nothing, concluded it was an imaginary lion, only in the idea of Eaco (the name of the Hottentot who had given us the intelligence), who having lately lost a very good mistress, killed by one of those animals, was in continual dread of them.

"Her habitation being on the skirts of a wood, one gloomy night the family was awakened by the lowing of the cattle, in an inclosure at a small distance from the house: they immediately seized their fire-arms, and running to the spot, found a lion had broken through the fence, and was making dreadful havock among the cattle. It was only necessary to enter the enclosure, and fire, to kill the animal; but neither of her sons, servants, or slaves, had sufficient courage to attempt it. The undaunted matron, therefore, entered alone, and armed with a musket, approached the scene of carnage: the darkness of the night prevented her perceiving the animal till she was close to him, when she courageously fired, but was so unfortunate as only to wound him; he instantly rushed upon her: the screams of the unfortunate mother brought her sons to her assistance. Furious, desperate, distracted, they flew upon the tremendous animal, and killed him, though too late to save her, and both fell breathless on the mangled body of their parent. Exclusive of the deep wounds she had received from the fangs and talons of the ferocious savage, he had bit one of her hands off at the wrist. Assistance was ineffectual; she died the same night amidst the vain lamentations of her pusillanimous sons and servants.

"The remembrance of this scene had made so deep an impression on the mind of Eaco, and filled him with such apprehensions, that he had frequently teazed his comrades with false alarms of being near the dens of lions, and being sure of seeing them in such and such a thicket, so that at last they paid little or no regard to his representations, and, in the present instance, acquainted us with his disposition, and advised me to order the horses forward, and to continue our route, as we were three days from any habitation, and our provisions nearly exhausted. The trembling Eaco at this instant cried, 'There, there!' when hearing a rustling among the bushes I hastily looked round, and saw the beast in the act of springing upon his prey, one of the Hottentots being within his reach, as swift as lightning he darted upon the poor fellow; but rather overleaping himself, in bringing him to the ground his fore-quarters extended so far over him, that his antagonist, with the utmost intrepidity and presence of mind, clasped him firmly round the middle, and pressed him to his breast, the animal was so situated that he could do him little or no injury; at this moment one of his comrades ran to his assistance, and clasped the muzzle of his piece to his ear, dispatched him instantaneously, and thus providentially delivered his fellow-servant unhurt from this imminent danger.

"This narrow escape, added to the loss of our man killed by the elephant, rather abated the ardour of our pursuit, and Monsieur began seriously to think of returning to the Cape, which we reached without any remarkable occurrences happening. In our way I shot an eagle of a species hitherto unknown, and considered as a great varity by my master: it was of a bright black, with a ring of burnished gold round his neck, and seemed to resemble the vulture as much as the eagle, though different in some instances. Hunger changes the eagle into a vulture; that is to say, when it is hungry it will feed on putrified carrion. It is a vulgar error that this bird only subsists by preying on others; for I have frequently seen eagles as well as other carnivorous birds, attracted by the offal of the beasts we had killed." He also related some particulars respecting the Hottentots, completely refuting the accounts of our geographical writers, who describe a most filthy custom used by the Hottentots at the marriage ceremonies, the priest being said to bestow publicly a urinary stream on the bride and bridegroom, in presence of all the assembled friends. The formalities of those marriages, he said, consisted in the promises they made each other to live together as long as they may find it convenient; the engagement made, the young couple from that moment are man and wife. They then kill some sheep, sometimes an ox, to celebrate this little holiday. The parents on both sides furnish the young couple with some cattle; they immediately apply themselves to the construction of a hut, forming an inclosure, and in getting together their little stock of necessaries. They live together as long as a good understanding subsists between them; for should any difference arise, which is not likely to subside, they make no scruple of separation, but part with as little ceremony as they met; and each, free to form fresh connexions, seek elsewhere a more agreeable partner.

In cases of separation, the effects of the married pair are equally divided; but should the husband, in his quality of master, insist on retaining the whole, the wife never fails to find those who will assert and defend her right; her family interests itself, nor are the friends of the man idle; so that sometimes, the whole horde is in a ferment; in the end they come to blows, and, as in other places, the conquerors give laws to the vanquished. The mother always has the care of the younger children, especially if they are girls, while the boys, who are able to follow their father, are sure to belong to him. These disagreements, however, are far from being common; and it is equally worthy of remark that they have no known law, or established custom, to which they can refer for the termination of their differences.

Among those Hottentots who are the most distant from the colonists, conjugal fidelity is held more sacred than among the polished offspring of refinement; though polygamy is not repugnant to the customs of the Hottentots, it is by no means common among them. They may take as many wives as they please; but whether from a love of peace, or any other motive, seldom have but one. Women are never known to cohabit with two men. Nature, that would ever have a man able to ascertain his own offspring, has wisely planted in the heart of a female Gonaquais Hottentot, an invincible aversion for such infamous prostitution; nay, so digusting is it to these people, that a husband, on a knowledge of the most trifling infidelity of his wife, might kill her, without fearing of incurring the reproach of his horde.

With ideas of honour such as these, the reader will the more easily be induced to discredit the assertions of many writers; that the Hottentots indulge in connexions of an incestuous nature. It being hinted that strong suspicions of this sort had been entertained of them, they shewed signs of the greatest detestation. "Do you take us for brutes?" said they, and immediately broke off all farther converse; nor could all we had to say prevail on them to forget the offence.

Chapter VI.

Having completely stored the ship with provisions and water, taken in six hundred casks of flour for the colony, and various other stores, the signal was made for the transports to be in readiness to get under weigh. I bade my new friend adieu, hastened on board, and the next morning we worked out of the bay. We had scarcely got a tolerable offing when a very heavy gale blew from the northward, and the sea soon ran mountains high. The vessel being deep loaded, we shipped some very heavy seas, which obliged us to lay too, near four-and-twenty hours.

I had often heard of the superstition of sailors respecting apparitions, but had never given much credit to the report: it seems that some years since a Dutch man of war was lost off the Cape, and every soul on board perished; her consort weathered the gale, and arrived soon after at the Cape. Having refitted, and returning to Europe, they were assailed by a violent tempest nearly in the same latitude. In the night watch some of the people saw, or imagined they saw, a vessel standing for them under a press of sail, as though she would run them down: one in particular affirmed it was the ship that had foundered in the former gale, and that it must certainly be her, or the apparition of her; but on its clearing up, the object, a dark thick cloud, disappeared. Nothing could do away the idea of this phoenomenon on the minds of the sailors; and, on their relating the circumstances when they arrived in port, the story spread like wild--fire, and the supposed phantom was called the Flying Dutchman. From the Dutch the English seamen got the infatuation, and there are very few Indiamen, but what has some one one board, who pretends to have seen the apparition.

About two in the morning I was awaked by a violent shake by the shoulder, when starting up in my hammock, I saw the boatswain, with evident signs of terror and dismay in his countenance, standing by me. "For God's sake, messmate," said he, "hand us the key of the case, for by the Lord I'm damnably scarified: for, d'ye see, as I was just looking over the weather bow, what should I see but the Flying Dutchman coming right down upon us, with every thing set--I know 'twas she--I cou'd see all her lower-deck ports up, and the lights fore and aft, as if cleared for action. Now as how, d'ye see, I am sure no mortal ship could bear her low-deck ports up and not founder in this here weather: Why, the sea runs mountains high. It must certainly be the ghost of that there Dutchman, that foundered in this latitude, and which, I have heard say, always appears in this here quarter, in hard gales of wind."

After taking a good pull or two at the Hollands, he grew a little composed, when I jokingly asked him, if he was afraid of ghosts? "Why, as to that, d'ye see,"--said he, "I think as how I'm as good as another man; but I'd always a terrible antipathy to those things. Even when I was a boy, I never could find it in my heart to cross a church-yard in the dark without whistling and hallooing to make them believe I had company with me, for I've heard say they appear but to one at a time; for now, when I called to Joe Jackson, who was at the helm, to look over the weather-bow, he saw nothing; tho', as how, I saw it as plain as this here bottle," taking another swig at the Geneva.

Having some curiosity to see if I could make out any thing that could take such an appearance, I turned out, and accompanied him upon deck; but it had cleared up, the moon shining very bright, and not a cloud to be seen; though, by what I could learn from the rest of the people who were on deck, it had been very cloudy about half an hour before, of course I easily divined what kind of phantom had so alarmed my messmate. The sea running very high, and the gale rather increasing, we continued to lay too, and in the morning found we had parted company with the rest of the transports, not one being discernable from the mast head.

The wind abating in the afternoon, and coming to the north-west, we bore away under a reefed fore-sail: and it continuing to blow a very strong gale, we jogged on in this manner about ten days, when the weather moderating we crouded all the sail we could make from this time till we made Van Dieman's land, off which we frequently saw in the night the sea covered with luminous spots, resembling lights floating on the surface, and I immediately imagined that it might have been some of these which the boatswain had seen through a passing cloud, and which be magnified into lanterns on a ship's lower-deck, as in some points of view they had very much that appearance.

Whether these shining spots proceed from the spawn of fish floating in small quantities, or from an animal of a jelly-like substance, called by the sailors, blubber, is not determined, though I am of the latter opinion; vast shoals of them surrounded the ship in the course of the day. Numbers of sea birds now hovered over us, such as albatrosses; gulls of various species; and a large black bird, greatly resembling a crow, but rather bigger. In the evening the horizon was beautifully illumined by the Aurora Austrealis, or southern lights: they were of a bright crimson, variegated with orange, yellow, and white streaks, continually changed their hues, and presenting a most sublime and animating picture.

The next morning at day-break, the man at the mast head cryed out, "Land, hoa!" which agreeable sound re-echoed through the ship; and it clearing up we found ourselves close in with it. It appeared a bold even shore, with some hills inland, pleasantly ornamented with fall strait trees, supposed to be cabbage or palm trees, from only having branches near the top.

We sailed along the coast for some leagues, in the course of which we saw some pretty deep bays. We now stretched off in order to get a good offing, and to weather some rocks about three leagues from the shore, being afraid of passing too near them in the dark.

At day-light they appeared about six miles on our leebeam. Here we perceived a number of scals playing and sporting alongside; they were in general of the size of a common dog, with a long head, tapered to the nose like a greyhound; they frequently raised themselves half the length of their body out of the water, turning round as it were to reconnoitre, and sometimes in their gambols leaped entirely out. We took our leave of these sportive gentry, and shaped our course for New Holland, before sunset lost sight of the land.

Chapter VII.

A FAVOURABLE slant of wind enabled us to make the land of New South Wales on the 12th of October, about eight leagues distant. We stood on till we were within about six or seven miles from the shore, and then ranged pleasantly along the coast. At noon we were abreast of a point of land, called Red Point, only ten leagues distant from Botany Bay. About two leagues to the southward of the Bay is a chain of chalky hills, over-topped by level land. On this land is a clump of trees, something like Postdown-hill, in the neighbourhood of Portsmouth. The wind springing up to the eastward, we stood from the land, under an easy sail, till daylight, when we were quite abreast of the Bay; and, at noon, on the 13th, came to an anchor in Port Jackson, about five or six leagues to the northward of it.

At ten o'clock the next morning the convicts were all ordered on shore; their appearance was truly deplorable, the generality of them being emaciated by disease, and those who laboured under no bodily disorder, from the scantiness of their allowance, were in no better plight. The boats from all the ships in the harbour attended, in order to land them; there were in all two hundred and fifty men, six women, and a convict's wife and child who had obtained permission to accompany her husband. We lost during the voyage thirty-two men. Upon their landing they were entirely new cloathed from the king's store, and their old things were all burnt, in order to prevent any infectious disorder that might have been in the ship, from being introduced into the colony.

From the report of the captain I had a most gracious reception from the governor; he told me that on account of my behaviour on board, he would place me in a situation that should render my exile from England as little irksome as possible, and that if I continued to deserve it I might rely on his favour and protection: for the present I might return on borrd, and as soon as any boat could be spared from the ship, it should convey me and what things I had, up to Paramatta, where a habitation should be provided for me. The next morning I received orders again to attend the governor at Sidney Cove, and to put my property in charge of a serjeant of marines, who came off in a large boat, and who was to see it safely lodged in the public store, till such time as I should be settled, and able to take care of it myself.

I took leave of my messmates with unfeigned regret, the captain himself accompanied me on shore, and waited on the governor with me. His excellency said, he had long wanted a proper person as superintendant of the convicts at Paramatta, that he had appointed me to that office, and that I should take charge of the farm-house there. When I was dismissed, the serjeant took me to his house, where I partook of a good fish dinner; and, it being some time before we could set off for my future residence, we took a walk round the Cove, where some considerable buildings have been erected, for the governor, the lieutenant-governor, the judge-advocate, and the greatest part of the officers.

The governor's house is of stone, nearly seventy feet in front, and makes a very handsome appearance. The houses of the officers are of brick; the rest are generally log houses, plaistered; the roofs are either shingled or thatched. Here is also an hospital, a good temporary building, and also barracks for the soldiers, and comfortable cabins for the officers, with gardens adjoining; but unluckily these gardens are not very productive, as the soil is very indifferent; and to this inconvenience must be added the depredations of rats and thieves. A mile or two from the Cove, the soil is considerably better, where the officers and others have little farms; there are also brick-kilns, and a pottery, both of which articles they would bring to tolerable perfection, were they possessed of the materials used to glaze their earthen-ware. I wonder there are not more stone buildings here, stone resembling that of Portland being at hand in great abundance, exceedingly soft, but hardens very much after it is wrought, and exposed to the weather.

Not being able to proceed 'till the morning, I slung my cot in a corner of the serjeant's house, and spent the evening with him; we rose at day--break, and re-embarking my effects, left Sidney Cove about eight o'clock in the morning, and arrived at Paramatta about noon. Two or three miles before you come to the town, the river is quite narrow, not more than six or eight yards across, and the banks so high that you can scarce see the face of the country. Where they were lower it had very much the appearance of a park or a gentleman's pleasure ground. In our progress we saw several kangaroos, but had a very imperfect glance of them; the grass being long, entirely hid them from our view, except when they were in the act of leaping.

We landed about a quarter of a mile from the town, and walked up to it; it is situated on an elevated spot in the form of a crescent: a strong redoubt is constructed, where there are very good barracks for a detachment of the military, which is always on duty here; as well to preserve good order and regularity among the convicts, as a check upon the natives, who from the distance to Sidney Cove might be tempted to molest the settlers, were there no armed force to protect them; they have little apprehension from the natives as they have never shewn any inclination to attack armed men; not that they are destitute of courage, but that they are perfectly convinced of the great and invincible superiority of our fire-arms. After a short walk we arrived at the house appropriated for me; it is a compact little cottage, with four rooms in it; the situation is most delightful, being in the midst of pleasant gardens, the convicts houses form a line in front, at some distance, they have each a small garden, and those who have been industrious seem very comfortable, as their day's work is not so hard as many working men's in England.

A servant who kept the house gave us some refreshment, after which I waited on the commanding officer of the troops on duty here, and presented a letter given me by the governor; my reception was as agreeable as I could expect, he told me that the next day he would cause the convicts to be mustered in my presence, and inform them of my situation, as superintendant, and would then give me some instructions necessary to regulate my future proceedings.

Chapter VIII.

IN the morning a general muster took place; when the whole were assembled, to the amount of near four hundred; they were informed by the officer of the trust the governor had been pleased to repose in me, and that any misbehaviour or disobedience of orders issuing from me would be as severely punished as tho' they proceeded from the governor himself: they were then dismissed to their several employments. I proceeded through the different gangs of people at their respective occupations; and found them much more attentive to their business and respectful to those over them than I could possibly have imagined. Some were employed in making bricks and tiles; others, building store-houses, huts, &c. a great number clearing the grounds, bringing in timber, and making roads. Others at their different callings, such as smiths, gardeners, coopers, shoemakers, taylors, bakers, attendants on the sick, &c. The hours of work are from sunrise to half past seven, when they breakfast; at half past eight they resume their work 'till half past eleven, when they are rung to dinner; at two they recommence their labours, and the setting of the sun is the signal that terminates their daily toil, and which is announced by the drum beating a retreat. In order to encourage the cultivation of gardens, Saturday is appropriated to clear away and cultivate spots of ground for themselves; and those who have been industrious now find the benefit, by having plenty of vegetables, which saves their salt provisions, and enables them to truck with the natives for fish. Indedendent of this advantage, those who rear the greatest quantities of vegetables and plants, receive premiums from the governor, who, at the proper season of the year, distributes seeds among them for that purpose. The women sweep round the huts every morning, and cook the victuals for the men, collect all their dirty cloaths, and return each man his respective linen, washed and mended, on the Sunday morning.

No person is excused from attending divine worship, which is performed every Sunday morning at eleven o'clock, when all the convicts are obliged to attend in clean linen, and, indeed, behave in a more orderly and devout manner than would be naturally expected: indeed, the indefatigable zeal and wise measures pursued by the worthy governor in the formation of this infant colony is beyond all praise.

I had some apprehensions that from my former situation in life I should have been exposed to many mortifications, although shielded by the protection of my office; but I saw few faces who recollected me, and those who did behaved in the most respectful manner. The greater part of those who came over with me were sent to Norfolk Island, and those that were left remained at Sidney Cove.

My business was chiefly to report the progress made in the different works carrying on at Paramatta: for which purpose I was furnished with abstracts from a kind of overseers or head men of the various gangs; and in less than a week, was as much at home, and as perfectly master of the business, as though I had been coeval with the colony.

From a necessary and well regulated discipline, the convicts who had come over in the first ships had been brought into the excellent order above described; but many severe examples were made ere they were reduced to order, and various knaveries and tricks played on the officers; but punishment never failed to attend the detection of their frauds. In the infancy of the settlement, a convict had industriously spread a report that he had discovered a gold mine, which at first gained credit, as the ore pretended to have been found had something of the appearance of gold ore.

The circumstance was as follows: one Dailey, a convict, had, he pretended, discovered a piece of ground which contained a considerable quantity of gold ore, some of which was produced, tried, and found to contain a small portion of gold. The governor was absent at this time on an excursion into the country: the report coming to the ears of the lieutenant-governor, he examined the pretended discoverer, who told his story with the greatest plausibility, and it was not doubted but an important discovery had been made. Dailey was interrogated as to the place, but refused to give the necessary information 'till the return of the governor, to whom he would give a full and satisfactory account of the discovery, on a promise that he would grant him what he should think equivalent to the importance of the discovery, and which he (Dailey) conceived a small compensation for so valuable an acquisition: the demand was, his own and a particular woman convict's enlargement, and a passage in one of the first ships to England, together with a sum of money. The lieutenant-governor told him, that unless he pointed out the spot he should consider him as an impostor, and order him to instant punishment, for daring to impose upon those officers to whom he had related the business. The dread of punishment disposed him to come too a little, though not without apparent reluctance: he proposed to the lieutenant-governor that an officer should be sent down the harbour with him, for the treasure, he said, lay in the lower part of the harbour, and near the sea shore: and he would shew the officer the exact spot; accordingly he was taken at his word, and an officer, with a corporal, and two or three soldiers, were sent with him; he pointed out the landing--place, whence he said it was but a short walk to the desired spot. They entered the wood, but had scarce got among the bushes, which were very thick, than he begged leave to turn aside, as though he had a pressing occasion; this was granted him: the officer continued waiting for him, but to no purpose; for as soon as he had got out of their reach he pushed off towards Sidney Cove by land, leaving the officer and his soldiers to beat their heels, and curse their credulity in letting him out of their sight.

The officer having dispatched the boat back on their landing, intending to return on foot, was left in no very enviable situation. Mr. Dailey reached Sidney in the afternoon, and informed the lieutenant-governor that he had left those whom he had sent down with him in entire possession of the gold mine; he then got a few things from his own tent, and disappeared. The party, after searching some hours for the cheat, marched round to the camp, where they arrived at dusk, heartily tired, and not a little chagrined at the trick the villain had put upon them.

The want of provisions soon brought the discoverer back to the settlement, and a severe flogging was the reward of his ingenuity; however he still persisted in having made the discovery which he before had mentioned, and his reason for quitting the officer who went with him was, that he was sure, if he made the discovery to the governor himself he should certainly get what he had demanded.

When the governor returned he was made acquainted with the business, and another officer was sent with him, although there was not a person in the colony who had the least faith in his assertions. The officer who now accompanied him informed him, on landing from the boat, that if he offered to quit him for an instant he would put him to death. This determination so terrified the gold-finder, that he acknowledged the imposture: he was then interrogated respecting the ore which he had produced. He confessed he had filed down part of a yellow metal buckle, and had mixed it with some gold filings from a broken ring, which he had got from one of the convict women, all which he had blended with some earth, and made it hard. The man who tried the ore had been a silversmith, and on separating the different parts he discovered a small quantity of gold contained therein: the cheat received a second punishment for his perseverance, and a recommendation to be very attentive to his duty, and not attempt any more tricks as he valued his neck.

Having a good deal of time on my hands, my attendance and inspection being generally finished in the forenoon, I frequently visited the farms of the settlers: these in general were convicts whose term of transportation had expired, and had had lands granted them, in the following proportions; thirty acres to every single man; fifty to the married ones; and ten more for every child; they received provisions and cloathing from the public stores for the first eighteen months: the necessary tools and implements of husbandry, with seeds and grains to sow the ground the first year; two young sow pigs were also given to each settler, and a pair or two of fowls. On those conditions twenty seven of them had commenced farming in the neighbourhood of Paramata, Prospect-hill, and at some ponds about two miles to the northward. At this time these settlements had little the appearance of farms; but as there were many very industrious and careful men among them, their stock soon began to thrive, and the face of the country shew evident signs of culture.

In my walks I often fell in with the kangaroos, of which there are great numbers: they are about the size of a common deer, of a dark tan colour; its head, I think resembles that of the mocock from the East Indies. The hind legs are much longer than the fore, and with them they leap and spring forward with amazing rapidity, their fore feet being seldom seen to touch the ground; and, indeed they are so very short, that it is not possible the animal can make great use of them in running; they have prodigious force in their tail, which is a principal part of their defence; when attacked, they strike a blow with this weapon sufficient to break the leg of a man, or the back of a dog; it also assists them in their springs which are truly surprizing. The native dog is much swiffer than the kangaroo, and will attack them with great courage: the chase is seldom of long duration, the kangaroo being soon tired, and is generally overtaken in less than a quarter of an hour. When seized if they have no opportunity of using the tail to advantage, they turn upon the dog, and catching hold with the talons of his fore-paws, he flies at and strikes his adversary with those of his hind feet, which are long, sharp, and of great strength; and if the dog is not assisted, it frequently happens that they get the better.

I have frequently seen male kangaroos, which, when sitting on their haunches, would measure at least from five feet eight to five feet ten inches in height: such a one would, I think, over-match any of the dogs; but I never ventured to try them singly. Having had several young native dogs given me from time to time, I take great delight in kangaroo hunting; it is not only an agreeable exercise, but produces a dish for the table, nearly as good as mutton; and, in the present dearth of live stock, is not an unacceptable present.

The native dog greatly resembles the Pomeranian breed: with their ears erect, they have a remarkable savage look, and are not unlike a wolf, both in size and appearance. There is no getting the better of their natural ferocity; for if you take ever such pains in rearing them, they will, at every opportunity, destroy the sheep, pigs, or poultry, nor do I think it possible to break them of this savageness of temper, so that they are of little or no use, except in hunting the kangoroo.

I had many opportunities of getting acquainted with several of the natives; and as I seldom saw them without giving them some trifle or other, soon became a great favourite with them, and mostly had one or other of them with me in my rambles. The men in general are from five feet six to five feet nine inches high; are rather slenden, but strait, and well made. The women are not quite so tall, rather lustier, but are mostly well made. Their colour is of a brownish black, of a coffee cast, but many of the women are almost as light as a mulatto: now and then you may meet with some of both sexes with pretty tolerable features; but broad noses, wide mouths, and thick lips, are most generally met with; their countenances are not the most prepossessing, and what renders them still less so, is, they are abominably filthy. They know no such ceremony as washing themselves, and their skin is mostly smeared with the fat of such animals as they kill, and afterwards covered with every sort of dirt; sand from the beach, and ashes from their fires, all adhere to their filthy skin, which never comes off, except when accident, or the want of food obliges them to go into the water. Some of the men wear a piece of wood, or bone thrust through the septum of the nose, which, by raising the opposite sides of the nose, dilates the nostril, and spreads the lower part very much. Many of them want the two front teeth on the right side of the upper jaw: and I have seen several of the women who have lost the two first joints of the little finger of their left hand, a circumstance which I have never been able to discover the meaning of. This want of the little finger I observed in elderly women; in girls of eight or nine years old; in young women who have had children; and in those who have had none. I have also observed that the finger has been perfect in individuals of all ages and descriptions. They have, in general, good teeth; their hair is short, strong, and curly; and they having no method of combing or cleaning it, it is always filthy and matted the men's beards are short and curly like the hair of their heads. They all go entirely naked, men, women, and children, and seem to have no fixed place of residence, but lay down wherever night overtakes them. Cavities in the rocks on the sea shore, are places they usually seek to shelter themselves from the wind and rain; and they mostly make a good fire before they go to sleep, by which means the rock round them becomes heated, and retains its warmth a considerable time, like an oven; and spreading a little dried grass they lie down and huddle together.

The men are generally armed with a lance, and a short stick which they use in throwing it; this stick is about a yard long, flat on one side, and a notch in one end, the other is furnished with a flat shell fixed into a split in the stick, made fast with a strong gum, which, when dry, is as hard as flint: on the flat side of the stick they place the lance, the but end of which rests against the notch in the throwing stick: poising the lance thus fixed in one hand, binding it with the fore-finger and thumb to prevent its slipping off; keeping fast hold of the throwing stick, they hurl the lance with considerable force, and tolerably true, to distance of seventy or eighty yards. Their lances are in general about ten feet long; the shell fixed on the throwing stick is intended for sharpening the point of their lance, and various other uses. Although they throw their lances with considerable velocity, I should think it no very difficult matter, being on one's guard, either to parry or get out of the way of them.

When they are upon hostile expedition, they paint their faces and bodies with red and white streaks, as if they intended to strike terror by their death-like appearance: some are mere lines drawn without attention or method; others with the greatest nicety and exactness. At a few paces distance some have the appearance of being accoutered-with cross belts: others with white circles round their eyes, and several horizontal lines across the forehead; others, again, have narrow white lines across the body, with a broad streak down the middle of the back and belly, and a single line down the arm, thigh, and leg. Being commonly marked with white, their black skins are seen very conspicuously between the lines, and, at a short distance takes very much the appearance of a skeleton, and which, I suppose, is what they intend to represent. The colours they use are chiefly red and white, the first of which is a kind of ochre, or red earth, which is found here in abundance; the latter is a fine pipe-clay, great quantities of which are used in the potteries established in the colony. The bodies of the men are much scarified, particularly about the breast and shoulders; and although not very regular, yet are considered as ornamental.

Chapter IX.

THE warriors thus armed and painted, range themselves in a line, with each a green bough in their hand, as a token that they do not mean to use force, unless obliged thereto, in their own defence, or in case their difference cannot be settled by an amicable agreement; a long parley generally ensues, and concession on both sides for the most part terminate their bloodless campaign.

Building themselves habitations never seem to have entered their imaginations, or any place to shelter them from the weather, though they have plenty of the most inclement; their indolence and want of foresight in this particular would be fatal to them, were it not for the liberal hand of nature, who has so abundantly supplied the sea shores with soft crumbly rocks, which, for the most part, are excavated by the washing of the sea, so as to form caves of very considerable dimensions, sometimes fifty or more of them find a comfortable lodging in one of these caves. In the woods where there are no rocks, they strip the bark off several trees, and cutting them into slips, fasten and interlace them to four stakes drove in the ground, bending broad pieces of the bark over the top to shelve off the rain: these commonly hold a family; and as the weather is very cold in the winter months, they find it necessary to huddle very close for the benefit of the warmth, to which each individual mutually contributes a share. These huts are only used when they are out a kangaroo hunting; for in that season they employ themselves wholly in the woods.

Most of the large trees are hollow, by decaying at the heart; and when the opossum, kangaroo, rat, squirrel, and various other animals which inhabit the woods, are pursued, they commonly take shelter in these trees. In order therefore to make sure of them, wherein they seldom fail, when they find them in the tree, one man climbs to the top, which is performed with wonderful dexterity, in the following manner: they cut notches in the bark about an inch deep, which is a kind of rest for the ball of the great toe; the two first notches are cut before they begin to climb, the rest as they ascend at such distances from each other, that when both feet are in the notches, the right is raised nearly as high as the middle of the left thigh; when they are raising themselves the hatchet is held in their mouths, that they may have the use of both their hands; and when making the notch the body rests on the ball of the great toe; the fingers of the left hand are also placed in a notch cut on the side of the tree, should it be too large to admit their clasping it sufficiently with the left arm to keep their body firm and close to it. In this manner they ascend, with wonderful agility, trees fifteen or twenty feet in circumference, sometimes sixty or seventy feet before they come to a single branch.

Being arrived at the top, or the place he judges the most convenient, he takes his seat with his club or stick in his hand, another person below makes a fire and fills the hollow trunk with smoke, which obliges the animal to attempt its escape, either upwards or downwards, but which ever way it takes, it is almost certain of destruction, as they very seldom escape. In this manner they employ themselves, and get a livelihood in the woods. They, sometimes, when many of them are hunting together, set fire to the country for several miles in extent; this is for the purpose of disturbing such animals as may be within the circle of the conflagration: thus the affrighted animals, confounded, singed, and half--smotherod, fall an easy prey to their persevering and sanguinary adversaries.

These fires, it is supposed, are sometimes intended to clear that part of the country through which they have occasion to travel, of the briars and thorns, from which, being naked, they suffer great inconvenience. The fires which are frequently seen in the summer time, account also for an appearance which very much puzzled the first settlers; this was, that more than two thirds of the trees in the woods were very much scorched with fire, some were burnt quite black to the very top; the cause of this occasioned great difference of opinion, but it is now evident that it was occasioned by the fires which the natives so frequently make, and which often reach the highest branches of the trees; I at first conjectured it to be the effect of lightning, but upon examining farther, it appeared too general to have been caused by such an accident.

Opossums are very numerous here: they partake a good deal of the kangaroo, in the strength of their tail, and make of its fore legs, which are very short in proportion to the hinder ones; like that animal it is provided with a false belly for the safety of its young in time of danger, and its colour very much resembles that of the common English rat; it is of the size of a small cat, and very inoffensive. There are a variety of other animals of different sizes, from the oppossum down to our implacable enemy, the field rat, all of which in some shape or other, partake of the kangaroo and opossum. I have caught several rats with their pouch full of young ones, formed exactly in their legs, claws, and tail, as the above animals. One would almost conclude from the great resemblance of the different quadrupeds found here, that there is a promiscuous intercouse between the different sexes of all those various animals. This strange similarity does not attach solely to quadrupeds, for the finny inhabitants of the sea are in the same predicament, their variety is truly astonishing; most of them partake in some degree of the shark, and it is no uncommon thing to see the head and shoulders of a skait to the hind part of a shark, or a shark's head to the body of a large mullet, and what is more astonishing, sometimes to the flat body of a sting ray, or holibet.

Nature seems equally playful in the feathered tribe, the parrot is the most common. I have shot several, with the head, neck, and bill of the parrot, and with the same beautiful plumage of those parts for which that bird here is distinguished; a tail and body of different make and colour, with long delicate feet and legs, which is quite the reverse of the parrot kind. There is also a bird with the feet and legs of a parrot, whose head, neck, make, and colour, are like the common sea-gull, with the wings and tail of the hawk. Neither is this confined to the animal creation; for here are trees-bearing three different sorts of leaves; others bearing the leaf of the gum tree, with the gum exuding from it, and covered with bark of a very different kind.

The country abounds in birds of numberless species: those of the parrot kind, such as the macaw, cockatoo, Jory, green parrot, and paroquets of different species and sizes, ornamented with the most gay and luxuriant plumage that can be conceived. The common crow is no stranger here, but is found in considerable numbers: the sound of their voice and manner of croaking is widely different from those in Europe. Hawks are in great plenty: pigeons, quails, and a great variety of small birds; but I have not seen any with an agreeable note.

There is also a very large bird, but it is not very common at first they were taken for the ostrich, as they did not fly when pursued, but ran so exceedingly fast that a strong native dog could not overtake them: I shot one of them, which measured upwards of two yards and a half from its feet to the upper part of its head. The difference between this bird and the ostrich is in its bill, which is narrower at the point; and it has three toes, which is not the case with the ostrich, as I had an opportunity of seeing several of them at the Cape. It possesses one singularity by which it cannot fail of being known, which is, that two distinct feathers grow out from every quill. Its flesh, though not the most tender grained, is far from unacceptable: it resembles, when raw, neck beef; and a side-bone of this bird makes an excellent dinner for half-a-dozen. The crow, I think, relishes equally as well here as the barn fowl in England. I have sometimes, when on a shooting excursion, fallen in with the black swan: the extremity of their wings are white, and all the rest of their plumage a bright black: its bill a pale pink, or crimson: they are of the size of the common white swan, and are a delicate appendage to the table.

A prodigious quantity of bats have made their appearance during these two last years; they are generally seen about Rose Hill towards the close of the evening: the head of this bat very much resembles that of the fox; the wings of many of them extend four feet from tip to tip. I have one of them that will eat out of the hand, and is as domestic in the house as a cat. Their smell is rank and offensive; and numbers having perished from the extreme heat of the weather, and fallen into the water about Rose Hill, rendered it undrinkable for some days.

There are as many different species of insects as of birds; the centipedes, spider, ant, and scorpion; the generality of these vary but little from those described as inhabitants of most parts between the tropics: the ant possesses not only the greatest portion of industry, but also of courage; an insult is never offered them with impunity: they are of various sizes, from the common European ant to near three quarters of an inch in length; they are also of different colours, as black, white, yellow, and red; the most formidable of which are the red-coated gentry: whenever it happens that they are disturbed by any person, or beast treading on their nests, which are constructed just beneath the surface, with numberless small passages, or outlets, they sally forth in myriads and attack the ill-fated and unconscious offender with astonishing intrepidity, and even continue their pursuit to a considerable distance; their bite, if not venomous, is attended with the most acute pain for some time: one species of them build their nests against a tree, of the size of a bee-hive; another kind raises mounts of earth with prodigious industry to the height of four feet.

The spider of this country nearly approaches the ant in point of industry; the smallest of these are larger than auy I ever saw in England; they spread their web in the wood between the trees, generally to the distance of ten or a dozen yards, and weave them so strong that small birds are frequently entangled therein. The silk of which the web is composed, when wound off in a ball, I think is equal to any I ever saw in the same state from the silk-worm; it is of the same colour, a pale yellow, or straw colour; of reptiles, there are snakes from the smallest I have ever seen in England to the length of eleven feet, and as thick as a man's leg; also lizards of various kinds and sizes.

A great variety of beautiful plants and flowers abound in this country; but being unacquainted with the science of botany I am consequently unqualified to descant on their different properties; we find wild spinage, parsley, and sorrel, but not in sufficient quantities to flatter ourselves with the hope of deriving any considerable advantage therefrom.

Exclusive of the plantain, banana, and other tropical fruits, here are some peculiar, I believe, to this country; that which they call the mizzabore greatly resembles our cherry, its taste is very insipid, and it varies but little from another fruit, similar in its appearance, but something smaller, and which is also found in abundance; there is also a third sort, which also resembles the former two; though there is so great a similarity between these fruits, it is remarkable that the trees which bear them are of very different kinds and appearance. These berries have all the same insipidity, and are held in no estimation by our people; but there is another berry, of about the size of a currant and grows on a tree, the leaves of which are much like the broom: the juice of this fruit when ripe, is, perhaps, the purest acid in the world; it is extremely pleasant to the taste, and by the faculty held in great estimation as a most powerful antiscorbutic. It is an excellent acquisition in making tarts, jellies, and other delicacies in the confectionary and pastry department. There is another species of berries, which when ripe, is a clear red, of the size of a currant, and shaped like a heart; it has a most pleasant flavour, is a strong astringent, and if not taken in too great quantities is not unwholesome, many of the people having eaten of them very freely without any pernicious consequence.

Here is also a nut which acts as a violent purgative, and emetic, if eaten unprepared: it must be soaked seven or eight days in water, taking care that the water be changed every day. When it has been thoroughly soaked, it is then roasted in the embers; and when done it is not unlike a chesnut, and very palatable.

Chapter X.

ABOUT a twelvemonth before my arrival, the small-pox made its appearance and occasioned a terrible havock among the poor natives. It was truly shocking to find the coves of the harbour, which were formerly thronged with numerous families in tempestuous weather, now strewed with the dead bodies of men, women, and children. No vestige of this cruel disorder being visible in the countenances of any of the natives, it was reasonable to suppose they were never before infected with it, and of course ignorant of the method of treating this cruel ravager of the human species. The various attitudes in which the dead bodies were found afforded reason to believe that when any of them were indisposed, and the disorder assumed the appearance of the small-pox, they were immediately deserted by their friends and left to perish in their helpless situation for want of sustenance. Some have been found sitting with their heads reclined between their knees; others were leaning against a rock, with their head resting upon it. Two children, a boy and a girl, the boy about nine, the girl about two years older, were picked up during the prevalence of this disorder, labouring under its dreadful effects. Two old men, who were supposed the fathers of the children, were picked up about the same time, and carried to the hospital, where they were taken all possible care of; the men survived but a short time, but the children both recovered, and appeared perfectly satisfied with their change of living.

About this time a native, who I saw frequently at the governor's, and who was now as perfectly at his ease in company as if he had been bred in England, being decently cloathed, and managing his knife, fork, cup and saucer with great dexterity, was entrapped from his friends. Some officers were sent down the harbour, with two boats for the purpose of seizing any of the natives they could lay their hands on; the governor having found that no encouragement would induce them to pay a visit to the colony of their own accord; he therefore determined to get some of them into his possession, and by kind treatment prevail on them to bring their countrymen to repose more confidence in us--Arabanoo, the name of the native above alluded to, was taken in the following manner.

Being enticed near to the beach, by a display of various articles calculated to excite his curiosity and desire, and busily employed in admiring the presents that were given him, one of the seamen, stationed for the purpose, threw a rope round his neck, and in a moment dragged him to the boat; his cries brought a number of his friends to the skirts of the wood, from whence they threw several spears, but without effect. To pourtray the terror and dismay depicted in the countenance of this poor creature, would require the hand of an able artist: he believed he was to be put to instant death; but when he was assured by the officers that his life was safe, and they at the same time casting off the rope they had bound round his neck and fixing it to his leg treated him with so much kindness that he gradually became cheerful. On his arrival at the governor's house he had an iron shackle put round his leg to prevent the possibily of an escape; this he was taught to consider as a bang-ally, a term in their language, used for a decoration of any kind; and it was no very difficult matter to bring him into the belief of this, as it was not uncommon to see some of the convicts ironed in the same manner, as a punishment for the crimes they had committed in the colony.

Arabanoo, from the kind treatment he experienced, was soon reconciled to his situation, and the iron becoming troublesome, galling his leg, it was taken off, and he was permitted to go where he pleased. The names of the different gentlemen who took notice of him were soon familiar to him, and he would call them with great facility--He was a very good tempered fellow, of about thirty years of age, well made, and on the whole not an unhandsome figure.

The intentions of the governor was however frustrated for a time; poor Arabanoo, ere he could bring about a good understanding with his countrymen, was attacked with the small-pox, which, not withstanding every possible means was used by the faculty for his recovery, he only lived till the crisis of his distemper.

Frequent indications of hostilities, as well as the missing of several of the convicts, who were supposed to have been murdered by the natives, made the governor exceedingly regret the fate of poor Arabanoo, who, had he lived, might have prevented much of this hostile disposition towards us, as he would have understood enough of our language to have communicated whatever we desired; he could have made them understand that we wished to live with them on the most friendly footing, and to promote, as much as in our power, their comfort and happiness.

The children had recovered from the small-pox, and were perfectly happy in their situation, but were then too young to be of service in reconciling their country-men to us; they very soon understood almost every thing that was said, and could also make themselves tolerably well understood: but the governor was still determined, if possible, to get a man or two into his possession, who might be taught enough of the language to render them useful negociators.

Accordingly some officers and a party of men were sent on this expedition, in an armed boat; they proceeded to the north side of the harbour, where they saw two of the natives walking on the beach; a plan was soon formed to entice them to conversation; a few large fish were held up, and an officer who spoke some words of their tongue, hailed them, which had the desired effect. The men advanced unarmed, with much confidence, and readily took the fish that was presented them. The boat was lying afloat, and five or six seamen on the beach nearly surrounding them; when the officer in the boat observing the opportunity favourable, made the signal to secure them; in an instant they were tripped up, and tumbled into the boat, ere they had time to look around. They called out to their friends the moment they recovered their recollection, and a considerable number appeared from the woods, and many spears were thrown, one of which pierced through the gunwale of the boat: the party pulling off instantly, and the people presenting their fire-arms, they halted, not daring to venture any farther attack. The two prisoners were made fast to the thwart of the boat on being put on board; but having got a good distance from the shore, their hands were loosed, and they were only secured by one leg. When they were landed at Sydney Cove, the residence of the governor, many people prompted by curiosity, went to see them; among whom were Abaroo, and Nanbarre, the two children before mentioned: the moment they saw them their eyes sparkled with joy; they called them by their names: the children were also known to them; and by their easy and apparently satisfied behaviour tended greatly to calm their apprehensions.

They discovered that one of the men they had taken was a chief of the tribe of Cardigal, named Coalby; he was about thirty-five years of age; the other, about twenty-five, was called Banalong: he was a smart, active, good-looking young man, of a lively pleasant disposition. His fellow prisoner appeared a check upon the volatile temper of Banalong, who, in his presence was always sedate and grave, and paid great deference to him; but no sooner was Coalby out of sight, than all his gravity forsook him, and he was as merry and good-humoured as though he had been all his life in the colony. They were treated with the utmost kindness; but lest they should attempt an escape, they wore each of them an iron on one leg, with a piece of rope spliced to it, and a man was ordered for each, who was to be responsible for their security. Wherever they went they were accompanied by their leaders; holding one end of the rope.

They had been taken near three weeks, when they appeared so well satisfied with their treatment, that their keepers began to be under very little apprehensions of their attempting to get from them; this security they did not fail to avail themselves of: accordingly one evening about dusk, their guards sitting within the door of their hut, eating their supper, Banalong being also in the hut in like manner employed, Coalby seated without the door, pretending to be also eating his supper, unslipped the rope from the shackle, leaving the other end fast in the keeper's hand, who had not the least suspicion of what was going forward: he was over the paling of the yard in an instant. The noise he made in leaping the paling roused those within, but too late; the fugitive gained the wood in spite of an immediate pursuit, and joined his friends. Banalong was much more cheerful after Coalby's departure, which confirmed the conjecture, and the children's report, that he was a chief, and consequently Banalong stood in great awe of him.

This man had several names; but the one he usually went by was Banalong: he is a stout well made man about five feet six inches high; he is dark black, large feathered, and has a flat nose; his hair is the same as the Africans, but very coarse and strong; he is very good humoured, of a lively and pleasant disposition, and seldom angry at any jokes that are passed on him; he readily imitates the actions and gestures of every person in the governor's family, and generally sits at table with the governor, whom he calls beanga, or father, and he in return, calls him doorow, or son: he is under no restraint, nor does he appear aukward in eating; and considering the savage state from which he has so recently emerged, he may be deemed a polite man, as he performs the ceremonies of bowing, drinking healths, returning thanks, &c. with the most scrupulous exactness. He is very fond of wine, but cannot bear the smell of spirits, although they have often tried to deceive him, by mixing very weak rum or brandy and water, and giving it him for wine and water, but he instantly discovers the deception, and is very angry on these occasions: he generally accompanies the governor in his walks, who to inspire him with confidence, always takes off his small sword, and puts it on him, and he is much pleased with this mark of distinction. His dress is a jacket, made of coarse red kersey, and a pair of trowsers; but on Sundays he is dressed in nan-keen. The governor's reason for making him wear the thick kersey is that he may be so sensible of cold as not to be able to go without cloaths. He sings when asked, but in general his songs are of the mournful strain; he keeps time by throwing his arms backward and forward. Whenever desired to dance, he does it with the utmost readiness; his gestures at first are very slow, and regulated by a low dismal tune, which quickens as the dance advances, 'till at length he throws himself into the most violent attitudes, shaking his arms, and striking the ground with great force, which gives him the appearance of a madman. It is very probable that this part of the dance is used as a kind of defiance, as all the natives which were seen when the governor first landed at Port Jackson, always accompanied this sort of dance to their vociferations of "waroo, waroo!" Go away, go away!

The kind treatment, and air of satisfaction which Banalong manifested for the space of a year after Coalby's flight, determined the governor to trust him with his liberty. Accordingly the shackle was taken from his leg, nor did he in the least seem disposed to leave the governor's house, or desert his new friends: he continued this behaviour with great success for several days, so that no person had the least suspicion of his leaving the colony; he, however, one evening, just as it was dark, stripped himself, and leaving the cloaths that had been given him behind, beat his march into the woods.

Both he and Coalby were frequently seen by the boats employed in fishing, and would even converse with the people, who earnestly invited them to return to Sydney; but no intreaties could prevail on them to accept the invitation.

The governor having received information that they were seen in a cove at the entrance of the harbour, he went thither, attended by several of the officers, but they were all unarmed, which ill-judged piece of confidence had like to have proved fatal to the governor. The particulars of this expedition were related to me nearly as follows:

The governor with some of the gentlemen of the colony, went down to the mouth of the harbour, in order to pitch on a spot proper to erect a landmark, to enable strangers the more readily to ascertain the harbour's mouth when at sea; on their return they were met by a boat, which had just landed a party of officers, who intended to take a survey of the shore as far as Broken Bay; the coxswain of the boat informed the governor, that one of the party (Mr. White, the surgeon) had seen Coalby and Banalong, and had had some conversation with them; and that they enquired after every person they had any knowledge of in the colony, and particularly the governor, and that they said they would go up to Sydney if he would come for them.

In consequence of this information, his excellency returned to the Cove, got some few presents for them, which he supposed would be acceptable; he also ordered four musquets into the boat, and immediately repaired to the spot where these men had been seen. When they arrived at the place, they found a number of the natives sitting round a fire, and near them lay the remains of a dead whale, which had been thrown ashore in a hard gale, and on which they had been heartily feasting. As soon as they were within hail, the governor stood up in the boat, and called for Banalong, and in their language asked where he was. Banalong instantly answered, "Here I am." His excellency then said, "I am the governor, your father;" which title he always gave the governor when he was at Sydney. After desiring two gentlemen to remain in the boat, and to have the musquets ready, upon examining which, two were found unprovided with flints, his excellency landed, and walked towards them with his arms extended, to shew them he was unarmed, and that they might be under no apprehensions for their safety: they appeared very backward in coming to a nearer conference; however, he continued approaching them 'till he entered the wood; one of them, possessed of more assurance than his comrades, after frequently repeating the words "Governor, father," ventured to shake hands in a friendly manner. His excellency then returned to the boat, and ordered one of the people to bring some wine, beef, bread, and a jacket or two which had been brought on purpose, and returned to them with these presents. On his shewing a bottle, one of them called out, "Wine, wine!" two of them immediately advanced, took the things, and drank a little of the wine: the governor also gave them two or three knives; he then returned to the boat, and told the gentlemen that remained in her that he had not seen either Coalby or Banalong, and that his mind was not altogether satisfied with regard to their pacific intentions: at the same time desiring them to stay by the boat, and give a look out, and be ready in case of alarm. He then went towards them, accompanied by Captain Collins. The officer in the boat frequently heard one of the natives call to Banalong, and acquaint him with the observations he made upon those who were in the boat, which was kept afloat upon her oars; presently after one of the people came down from the governor, and acquainted Mr. Waterhouse, the officer left in the boat, that both Coalby and Banalong were among them, and asked for him, and that Governor Philip desired he would join them. He immediately accompanied the messenger to the governor, whom he found with Captain Collins, in close conversation with two of the natives, who were unarmed: Mr. Waterhouse went up, but did not recognize Banalong 'till he was pointed out to him, so much was he altered, nor could he then persuade himself that he was the same. On the question being repeatedly asked, where was Banalong, he grew rather impatient, and was going off; however, a bottle being shewn him, and being asked the name of it, he readily answered, "The king;" having observed when at the governor's house, his majesty's health drank in the first glass after dinner, and had been taught to repeat the word before he drank his own glass, he imagined the liquor was called the king; and when he afterwards came to know it was wine, yet he would frequently call it king. This convinced the gentlemen that he was no other than their old acquaintance Banalong; and every method was tried to induce him to go down to the boat; but he always retired when any one approached nearer than he wished, so that they gradually got out of sight of the boat, when about a dozen of the natives placing themselves in a situation to prevent any surprize. Banalong and Coalby came among the gentlemen, and asked various questions relative to different transactions which had occurred at the settlement during their residence there. Banalong took Mr. Watherhouse round the neck, Coalby shook them all by the hand; a jacket being presented to him he was puzzled how to put it on, and begged one of the gentlemen to do it for him: Banalong had a very fine spear in his hand, which the governor asked him for, but he would not part with it. During all this time the most perfect harmony and friendship seemed to subsist among the whole party; but the governor, perceiving upwards of twenty of them closing round his party, proposed returning to the boat, telling Banalong that he would shortly return, and bring him and Coalby a couple of hatchets, which pleased them extremely. The governor then went down to the beach, and the officers left in the boat came on shore; the boat's crew with the arms remained in the boat: as the natives, by continuing their position, indicated some remaining symptoms of distrust, his excellency was afraid of alarming them. Banalong was very cheerful, and appeared transported at the sight of so many of his dear friends, as he termed them, incessantly shaking hands all round. He pointed out a small fire near them, and said he would sleep there till their return. They were very merry on their escape, and told them how Coalby got rid of the shackle by which he had been secured when at the settlement, and that if they had meant to keep them, they should never "Nangora,"--Fall asleep.

The governor and his party now began to move towards the boat, when a stout native, who had been seen standing at a distance, approached: at first he shewed strong indications of fear, which soon subsided on his being treated in the same familiar friendly manner as Coalby and Banalong, and he became tolerably conversable. He shewed a wound which he had received in the back with a spear; this also put Banalong upon shewing that he had also been wounded in different parts of the body since he quitted the settlement; one was thro' the left arm, made with a spear; another dangerous one over the left eye, not healed: these wounds he said, were received in a rencounter with a neighbouring tribe near Botany Bay.

The party still proceeding towards the beach, were detained by Banalong, who continued teazing them about the hatchets that were to be sent him; and he pointed out the stout native, who had retired about thirty yards distance, whom he appeared anxious should be noticed: the governor advanced towards him, and upon the savage indicating that he would not be approached, he laid down his sword, still going forward with extended arms, to assure him he was unarmed.

As the governor drew near, the native seized a spear that lay concealed in the grass, fixed it in his throwing stick, and for some moments appeared to stand on his defence. There being not the least reason to suppose he would throw it without provocation, his excellency continued to advance, calling out "Weree, weree," a term used by them when they wish a thing not to be done which displeases them: notwithstanding which the native discharged the spear with surprizing velocity, and immediately ran off. In their retreat to the woods many spears were thrown, but the only one which took effect was unfortunately the first, which struck our much loved governor: it entered his right shoulder just above the collar bone, and came out behind, about three inches lower under the blade bone.

The gentlemen near the governor concluded he was mortally wounded, and feared, from the number of armed men that began to shew themselves from the woods, that it would be impracticable for them to reach the boat. The governor, holding up the spear, which trailed on the ground, endeavoured to make his way to the beach, but its great length frequently stopped him; in this situation he desired some one to endeavour if possible to draw the spear out of his body, but it being barbed, it was found impracticable; they then with great difficulty broke it, and disembarassed him from the greater part; he then drew a pistol from his pocket, and discharged it at them, who from the apprehension of there being more fire-arms among the party, kept a respectful distance; and the governor, carried between two of the people, reached the boat without any farther molestation.

Immediately after their arrival at Sydney, the surgeon was sent for. Mr. Balmain, the first who arrived at the governor's house, after examining the wound, relieved every body from the most painful suspense, by assuring them, that alarming as the situation of the governor might appear, he did not apprehend any fatal consequences from it: he extracted the point of the spear, dressed the wound, and to the admiration of every body, in six weeks he was enabled to go about.

Chapter XI.

GOVERNOR Philip still desirous of being reconciled with the natives, did not harbour any resentment towards them on account of the late transaction, which he construed to have proceeded from a sudden impulse of fear rather than treachery, and had given the necessary directions that none of them should be fired at, or any ways molested, unless they provoked it by the throwing of spears, or other hostilities.

Nanbarre, the boy, who had now become a tolerable interpreter, attended some of the officers who were on a shooting excursion, near the spot where the accident to the governor had happened, a number of natives appeared on the eminence at a short distance; being asked who it was that threw the spear at the governor, they named a man of the tribe who dwelt to the northward; that his name was Carrigal. Nanbarre was also desired to enquire after Banalong and Coalby, when they pointed to some people at a distance--One of whom threw a a spear at an officer who asked for it: but evidently with no mischievous design, as he took care it fell where nobody was standing.

The girl, Abaroo, was in the boat, and pointing to one of the natives said it was her father, and was very desirous of going with them; she had arrived at an age, when her inclination began to tend towards the other sex, and with great naivete and innocence told the officers that she wanted to be married--As she had no opportunity of a connexion of that kind in the clergyman's house where she dwelt, and it would be a difficult matter to keep her against her will, it was judged most prudent to permit her to go where she pleased, and she was told that as soon as some new cloaths could be made for her, she should take them with her, with which assurances she was perfectly satisfied to stay some time longer; during which great pains were taken to instruct her in English, that she might be enabled to explain our intentions towards her countrymen.

The governor being sufficiently recovered to venture in a boat, went to the place where Banalong and his wife lived--he found several natives on the spot, who told him that they were out a fishing, Araboo was in the boat, and her father being among them, a hatchet and some fish were given him, and he gave the governor a short spear in return;

as the boat was pushing from the shore they perceived four canoes paddling towards them, in the foremost they perceived Banalong: the boat then lay too on her oars, and they landed from the canoes; as soon as Banalong had secured his, he approached the boat, holding up his hands to shew he was unarmed.

Upon which the party landed from the boat, and he very readily joined them; he asked the governor where he was wounded, and said that he had quarrelled with and beat the man who had wounded him--being told that he would be killed if he was caught, he seemed no ways concerned, but desired it might be done--several presents were made him, and he wanted some also for his wife; but being told that if she wanted them she must come and fetch them herself, in about half an hour she made her appearance; she was called Barangaroo, and appeared older than him: a petticoat and several little presents were given to the lady, and a red jacket with a silver epaulette, which Banalong used to wear when at the settlement, were given him, which delighted him exceedingly; he was asked if he would come and dine with the governor the next day, to which he readily assented, and said that he would bring his wife and some friends with him.

Notwithstanding Banalong did not visit the governor according to his promise, he frequently joined the different parties he fell in with, although they were well armed, and would without the least fear go to the long boat, though he always saw muskets in her; his wife was generally with him in the canoe, and he intimated that he still intended paying the governor a visit, but his suspicion of being detained apparently had not beeen entirely done away: however, the governor did not chuse to take him a second time by force, as he still entertained hopes that he would soon be reconciled to pass some of his time at Sidney, when he could be assured of being his own master, to go and come when he pleased.

At length his excellency's wishes were accomplished; as he was going to Paramata, a native was seen standing on one of the points of land, and as they rowed past him he was asked where Banalong was, when he pointed to an island called Memill[?], to which they rowed; as they drew near the rocks he came down to the boat, accompanied by his wife, without the least signs of fear or distrust. They greedily took some bread that was given them, and the boat soon after pushed off and left them; from the confidence now evinced by this man, there was little doubt but he would shortly trust himself at Sydney. Accordingly a few days after, as the governor was passing in his boat, Banalong called to him repeatedly from the opposite shore where he was with some of the officers; and the surgeon, in whom he placed great confidence, persuaded him to go over to the governor; he took three natives with him, who were: exceedingly pleased with the presents made them. It seems that Banalong's wife opposed his coming, and finding her tears and entreaties of no avail, flew into a violent passion, and broke a very fine fish-gig of her husband's, for which she would have received a hearty drubbing, had it not been for the interference of the surgeon, who took them back to their residence on the north shore.

Banalong appeared quite at his ease, and not under the the least apprehension of being detained; he promised when he went away to bring his wife over, which he did two days afterwards, accompanied by her sister and two other natives; they were followed by a third--Blankets and cloathing were given them, and each as much fish as they could eat. Banalong dined with the governor, and drank his wine and coffee as formerly--his excellency bought a spear of one them, and gave them to understand, that spears, lines, birds, or any thing they brought should always be purchased; and at the same time promising him a shield, for which he was to bring a spear in return--The next day a large party came over for the shield, but it was not finished; two of these men were owned by Araboo, as her brothers, and for whom she procured two hatchets, the most desirable present that can be given them--Banalong came the next day for his present; several of his comrades who accompanied him went away in a short time, but he staid to dinner, and left Sydney Cove, highly delighted with his shield, which being made of a good substantial hide, and covered with tin, was likely to resist the stroke of a spear. It being late in the afternoon before he thought of returning, his wife and sister, with two men, came over in their canoes to fetch him.

The girl who had been near eighteen months in the colony with the clergyman's wife, was so impatient to get away that at last it was consented to; and the very next day after she had left the settlement she was seen in the canoe naked; however, she put on her petticoat before the joined the glergyman and some others who went to visit her: she appeared much pleased with her liberty, and the boy, Nanbarre, who was of the party, wished to stay with the natives all night; he was accordingly left behind, but the next morning returned to the settlement, and having fared but indifferently did not seem inclined to renew his visit.

The natives now visited the colony daily; one morning Banalong came very early and breakfasted with the governor, and on taking his leave told him he was going a great way off, but should return in three days, with two young men who were with him; and it was conjectured that they were going to fight with some other tribe.

When Banalong returned from his expedition, he immediately waited on the governor, with whom he dined according to custom: after dinner he related the cause of his absence; that he had been to fight a man who had formerly wounded him; he said his shield was a good one, and that his spear had pierced the shield and arm of his antagonist: he also said that the people he had been to fight with had killed one of the convicts, who had been some time missing.

Governor Philip conjectured that the women were not treated with the greatest deference, in which conjecture he was certainly not much mistaken; for Banalong frequently beat his wife with great severity, altho' he professed great affection for her. He was often told that it was wrong and unmanly to beat a woman; but he only laughed at these remonstrances, and continued daily to visit the settlement, with his wife, children, and half a dozen of his friends: Coalby was generally one of the party.

Banalong, with his wife and children, now lived in a hut which the governor had built for them on the eastern point of the cove; they constantly had a number of visitors many of whom came daily to the settlement; and all of them becoming very fond of bread, which they got in exchange for a trifling article they brought, they soon found the advantage of coming amongst the settlers.

It had hitherto been the opinion that the custom of losing the front teeth was confined to the men, but a woman was also seen with the same mark, and two of them had the bottom of the gristle which parts the nostrils perforated; one of them was Barangaroo, the wife of Banalong, who never considered herself dressed but when her nose was dilated with a small stick, thrust through the septum or gristle of the nostrils. She is very strait and well-formed, her features well proportioned and pleasing, and though she goes entirely naked, there is such an air of innocence about her, that cloathing scarce seems necessary.

Araboo, the native girl, returned to the colony, after a few weeks absence, with some officers who had been down the harbour, and seemed perfectly happy in the opportunity of getting from the party she had been with. She said that she had lived three days with the young man she wished to marry, but that he had another wife, who was jealous of her, and had beat her; indeed evident marks of ill-usage appeared about her head, which was so much hurt that she was put under the surgeon's hands. Her favourite, it seems, had taken her part, and beat his wife in return; but matrimonial squables, which are always settled by the exercise of the cudgel, are very frequent, and the women in general treated very roughly.

Sixteen of the natives paid a visit to the governor one morning, and were regaled with fish for breakfast, to which they sat down in the yard in the utmost good humour: those who had not been there before were highly delighted with the novelties that surrounded them. Banalong who had been absent for some days, was of this party, and brought his wife with him; she appeared very ill, and had a fresh wound on her head, which he gave the governor to understand was because she had behaved ill, and in her ill-humour had broken a fish-gig and a throwing stick. The governor again reasoned with him on the subject of beating his wife, but to no effect; he said she was wicked, and therefore he had beaten her. When they had finished their breakfasts, his wife and another woman, a stranger, who had also been wounded by some of the men, went to the surgeon to have their heads dressed; when they returned, Banalong missing the governor, enquired for him, and said that he wanted to see him; upon which he was taken to his excellency, who was writing. Banalong seated himself, and appeared very much out of humour, frequently saying that he was going to beat a woman with a hatchet, which he held in his hand: it was impossible to divert him from his purpose, and after some conversation, he was going to take his leave, excusing himself from dining with his excelleney, as he was going to beat the woman; upon which the governor insisted on accompanying him; he made no objection to the proposal, though he was told that he would not be permitted to beat the woman. They set off for the hut, the governor ordering a serjeant and a couple of marines to attend him, and the judge-advocate coming in at the time, went with them.

Though Banalong had said he would kill the woman, when they were endeavouring to persuade him not to beat her, it was not supposed that he harboured any such intention, not was it thought there would be much trouble to prevent his beating her; but lest he should in his passion strike her with the hatchet, which might be fatal to her, it was taken from him before they got to the hut, and as he appeared reluctantly to part with it, the governor gave him his cane; but his menaces and countenances made them believe even that too dangerous a weapon to trust him with, and it was accordingly taken from him.

When they came to the hut, they found several men, women, and children assembled; and notwithstanding Governor Philip endeavoured to single out the object of Banalong's displeasure, whom he was determined on protecting, the furious savage seized a wooden sword, and darted on his victim, a fine girl of about fifteen, who, on seeing him coming had hid her face in the grass; he struck her several blows on the head before the weapon could be wrested from him; he then seized a hatchet, but was prevented doing any farther mischief.

The fury which took possession of him when he found himself prevented from beating the girl is indescribable: the poor creature lay trembling in the grass, not daring to stir, and in momentary expectation of being put to death: he had got another sword, and was preparing to repeat his violence, but was laid hold of by the judge-advocate and the serjeant. The fracas being observed by the officers on board the Supply, they instantly went on shore armed, and took the poor girl without any opposition from the natives, who had all armed themselves the moment they saw the governor and his party interfere.

When the boat had taken the girl on board the Supply, the party returned to the governor's house, where they were joined by several of the natives; Banalong was of the number: after some time his passion subsided, and he grew calm. He was then given to understand that the governor was very angry with him for endeavouring to kill a woman: that it was a cowardly and unmanly action, and should it be known that he did kill her, or even beat her any more, he should be put to death himself; but threats had no greater effect on him than entreaties, and he complained bitterly of the injury done him by depriving him of his victim; saying, that she was his, that her father had wounded him over the eye, that she was of a wicked tribe, and that they should see he would kill her. When he was talked to by the judge-advocate, and told that if he killed the girl the governor would kill him, he pointed with his fore--finger to the parts of the head, breast, and arms, where he said he would wound her before he cut her head off; in this resolution he returned home, and the girl was brought from the Supply to the governor's, accompanied by a young man whom Banalong had desired to remain with her. The attention paid her by this young native made every body conclude he was her husband, though he had not been seen to murmer or express any signs of dissatisfaction when her life was in danger.

Two days after Banalong returned to Sydney, apparently in great good humour; he said he would not beat the girl any more, but that he had been obliged again to chastise his wife, and had wounded her on the head, and that he had received a wound on the shoulder from a club in return. On being told to go to the hospital to have it dressed, as well as his wife's head, he refused, saying, that the surgeon would kill him, and that he was afraid of sleeping in his hut, lest he should shoot him in the night; though, to shew he was not afraid of meeting him openly, he went once or twice into the room where he had left his spear, brought it, and shook it by way of defiance. Governor Philip assured him that no harm was intended him, unless he killed the girl, or threw spears at the English. As soon as he was satisfied that the surgeon was still his friend, he agreed to go to him for a plaister for his shoulder; but his excellency, desirous of being present at their meeting, sent for Mr. White; Banalong received him as usual, giving him part of what he was eating, and went with him to the hospital; after which he went to his house, and the girl being there against whom he had lately been so incensed, he took her by the hand, and spoke to her in a friendly manner. Barangaroo, who was present, was so exasperated at her husband's attention to the girl, that it was with great difficulty she could be prevented from doing her a mischief with a club she had snatched from one of the by-standers: nor did Banalong seem disposed to prevent her, till desired by Mr. White, when he gave her a sound slap on the face: she not being able to vent her passion on the girl, burst into tears, and went to the governor's; the girl was taken there for greater security, and was followed by several men.

Governor Philip ordered her to be put in a room occupied by one of his maid servants, at which Banalong seemed greatly pleased, and begged him to let the same young man stay with her; in the mean time his wife grew quite outrageous, and used many threats; she had got her husband's spears, which she would not part with, till forced from her by one of the soldiers, from whom Banalong wanted to take them, saying he would give them to the governor himself; upon which they were delivered to him, and he immediately gave them as he promised, begging that they might be lodged in the house: this shewed he placed some confidence in Governor Philip, notwithstanding, he was very violent against those who prevented him entering the house, and threatened to knock them down with his club, though a file of soldiers were drawn up in the yard, and he knew that they had orders to fire on the least violence being offered. One of the natives, who was generally his companion, seemed ready to support him in any attempt he might be disposed to make. They were all turned out of the yard except Banalong-- Barangaroo was also turned out with the rest, but he staid dinner, and behaved with as much indifference as if nothing had happened. In the evening, when they were going, an unexpected scene took place; the native who had remained with the girl would stay no longer, and the girl forced her way out of the room to go with Banalong; she was brought back, and told she would be beat if she went with him, but he said he would beat her no more, and begged that she might be permitted to accompany him: that Barangaroo would be reconciled to her, as her passion was over, and she was now very good.

The governor was fully persuaded that Banalong would keep his word, but the general opinion was against him, and that the girl would be sacrificed; but the next morning he returned to dinner, and said he had sent her to her friends, which was afterwards confirmed. How he got this girl into his possession could never be learnt; she appeared about fifteen, and when she went away her wounds were in a fair way of doing well; fortunately for her the weapon Banalong first caught hold of was a boy's wooden sword, and made of very light wood; but they pay little attention to wounds, and even those which have been deemed dangerous by the surgeons, do not seem to require the attention of closing and keeping them clean; which shews that they must be of an excellent habit of body.

Chapter XII.

Shortly after, the governor having occasion to visit Paramatta, Banalong said he would accompany him; accordingly they set out, and stopped at the point, in order to take his wife into the boat, but she refused, and also persuaded him to change his mind. On his excellency's return to Sydney, he was told that this party had been lamenting the loss of a brother, who had been killed by one of the Camaragals; the women cried violently, but their grief was of no long duration; and Banalong went away with the officers, who, hearing the cries of women, had gone to the hut to learn the cause. As they proceeded down the harbour, looking after a small boat that had been lost with five convicts, he begged them to land him on the north shore, in order, it was supposed, to collect his friends, to go and revenge his brother's death. They found the wreck of the boat, and one of the bodies: and being seen under sail when it blew a gale of wind, it was supposed that the people were ignorant of the management of her, and she had been driven ashore among the rocks. The natives were very alert in saving the oars and other articles that were driven ashore, and Coalby exerted himself greatly on the occasion, and saved the seine which was entangled among the rocks, for which he was rewarded with some cloathes, and a couple of blankets; the rest of them had also some small present; but let you cloathe these people ever so well, they generally return naked the next day; for of all the things that had been given to Banalong, very little remained in his possession; he had, he said, sent his shield, and most of his cloathes, a long way off; but whether he had given them away, sold, or lost them, was equally uncertain.

The governor had built a small house at Paramatta, (the one I now occupy) and was going to remain there some time, when several of the natives were desirous of accompanying him, among whom were Banalong and Coalby. His excellency took three of them in his boat; but Banalong going to fetch his cloak, was detained by his wife; but as they were going out of the cove he appeared on the rocks, and got into the boat, in spite of her threats and entreaties. No sooner was the boat put off, than she went to her canoe, which was a new one, and stove it, and breaking the paddles, threw them into the water; she then went to the hut, probably with the intent of committing more mischief. Banalong endeavoured to pacify her, telling her he would not be more than one day absent; but all would not do, and he was put on shore. The party then proceeded to Rose-Hill, with Coalby and two other natives, none of whom ever opened their lips during the altercation; indeed, they are never known to interfere in any dispute which does not immediately concern themselves.

The natives slept that night at Paramatta, and though they wanted for nothing, yet the next morning were very anxious for returning; a boat was accordingly sent down with them, by the return of which it was generally expected that news would be received of Mrs. Barangaroo being again under the hands of the surgeon for her freaks; but to the surprize of every body, the next day they both made their appearance, and it seemed that he had not beaten her: whether he had withheld the usual correction from what had been formerly said to him by the governor, or from some other cause, could not be discovered; however, a reconciliation had taken place, and they both dined with his excellency, in great good humour. Every thing they desired was given them; but no sooner was the dinner ended than the lady wished to return, and Banalong said she would cry if they detained her, so that they were obliged to send a boat down in the evening with her.

On the return of the governor to Sydney, he learnt that his gamekeeper had been dangerously wounded by the natives with a spear. It appeared that he went out with three others, one of whom was a serjeant, and in the heat of the day they retired to a hut they had made with boughs, and laid down to sleep. One of them awaking, heard a noise in the bushes, which he supposed to be some animal; but on awaking his comrades, and coming out of the hut, four natives started up from among the bushes, and ran away with all their speed: the gamekeeper thinking he knew one of them, who had been at

Sydney, followed them without his gun, notwithstanding positive orders had been given for no one to trust himself with the natives unarmed, calling on them to stop, and he would give them some bread, and observing one who followed him to have a gun in his hand, desired him to lay it down, as it only frightened the natives, and they would do them no harm: he had now advanced about fifty yards before his companions, and was not ten paces from one of the natives, who stopped short, and finding they were unarmed, fixed his spear on the throwing stick in a moment, and threw it at the man nearest him: it entered his left side and penetrated the lower lobe of the lungs: it was barbed, and consequently could not be extracted till a suppuration took place. Immediately after throwing the spear, the native fled into the woods, and was seen no more.

They were eleven miles from Sydney when this accident happened, and it was with the greatest difficulty that the wounded man could be brought to the settlement. Being questioned whether he had provoked the natives to this violence, he desired to have the clergyman sent for, to whom he confessed he had been a very bad man; but at the same time declared that he had never killed or wounded any native, except once, when having had a spear thrown at him, he discharged his piece, loaded with small shot, and wounded the man that threw the spear; this declaration added to the testimony of those who were with him, left no room to doubt but that the native had taken the advantage of his being unarmed.

Banalong and Araboo repeatedly said that it was the tribes which lived about Botany Bay who threw the spears, and killed the white men, yet as it was evident that they generally received some provocation from our people, the governor was loth to proceed to extremities, whilst there was any possibility of avoiding it; especially as he had been at so much trouble in bringing them to repose some confidence in him; and a good understanding with them was essentially necessary to the happiness and prosperity of the colony.

Many of the natives now daily visited the settlement, and were all well received; it was no unusual thing for the mothers to leave their children behind them for several days, without ever enquiring after them; and if any of them were going where the children would be an incumbrance, they made no scruple of leaving them at Sydney, Banalong, Coalby, and two or three others took up their quarters three or four days in a week, and all joined in the same story, and desired those natives might be killed who threw the spears; but Governor Philip had his suspicions that there was a great deal of art and cunning in Banalong; he had lately been seen among those people he now wished to be killed, where he said they danced, and that one of them had sung a song in praise of his house, the governor, and the white men at Sydney; and he said those people would throw no more spears, as they were now all friends; this was but a few days after he was so solicitous with the governor to kill them all.

What was rather extraordinary, they all knew the man that threw the spear; they said his name was Pemulaway, of the Bejigal tribe: Banalong and Coalby said they would bring him to the governor; and went off the next day, as it was supposed, to Botany Bay; and his excellency, upon a report that a number of natives had been seen armed about the mouth of the harbour, went down to the Lookout; he met Coalby there, who returned to Sydney with him, but did not seem inclined to give himself any trouble about Pemulaway, but after dinner took his leave, saying he was going to Botany Bay to meet his wife. Banalong was absent several days; they said he was gone to assist at the ceremony of drawing a front tooth from some young men among the Camaragals, which gave rise to the idea that the tooth is exacted as a kind of tribute.

Araboo now resided with the Camaragals; when she left the clergyman's she promised to return with her sweetheart, and his wife: hence it appears evident that when they can procure two wives, the custom of the country does not prohibit their having them; though this custom seems very unreasonable, as the women bear no proportion to the men in point of number. It is generally believed that most of their wives are taken by force or surprize, from the tribes with which they are at variance; consequently, their enemies retaliate, and from the disproportion of the females to the males, must have been more successful in their Sabinical expeditions.

Spears being frequently thrown at the settlers, it became absolutely necessary that a stop should be put to it, though his excellency wished to do it with as little severity as possible, yet he was convinced that a severe example must be made to have the desired effect. Accordingly a party was sent out consisting of fifty privates, besides officers; they were directed to proceed to the spot were the man was wounded, and to search for the natives who dwelt thereabouts, some of whom were to be secured and brought prisoners, or if it was found impracticable to take them alive, they were to put half a dozen of them to death--Spears, and all other weapons which they happened to meet with were ordered to be destroyed and left on the spot, that they might see it was intended as a punishment inflicted on them--Particular attention was to be paid to the women and children, who were not to be molested on any account whatever; and as the governor wished to impress the idea that no deceit was ever practiced, and that they might depend on having protection whenever it was offered; he ordered that none of the party should hold up their hands, which is the signal of friendship; nor to answer such signal if made them by the natives; they have lately behaved with great insolence on several occasions; and a punishment inflicted on a few, might in the end be an act of mercy to many.

Notwithstanding the most vigilant endeavours, the party was not able to get near any of them, as they made off at their approach, and eluded the pursuit. They saw Coalby near Botany Bay, where he was fishing, at whom they fired several shot. They returned to Sydney without any success; but the governor being determined if possible to make an example of some of them, again sent the party with the same orders they had before received.--They left Sydney towards evening with the hope of surprizing some of the natives at their fires, but were disappointed, not a single native being seen during all the time they were out.

It was near a fortnight before Banalong made his appearance, when he brought his wife with him; he said he had been with the Camaragals, that several young men had undergone the operations of having their front teeth drawn, and tattooing, which is marking those scars which are considered as ornamental by the natives--These scars are made by cutting two lines through the skin, parallel to each other, with a sharp shell or flint, and then stripping off the intermediate skin; the operation is repeated till the wound rises considerably above the surrounding flesh, when it is suffered to heal over. These painful embellishments are not very common among the women. Banalong shewed a throwing stick which had been cut for the purpose of knocking out the front teeth; and it was generally supposed he had been employed in that office. He was on good terms with the Camaragals, and he said they were all good people: when he was asked if he had seen the man who threw the spear at the governor, he said yes, and had slept in the same cove with him; so that his former account of having quarrelled with, and beat him, was not believed. Barangaroo, who had been with him on this occasion, was painted in a different manner from what she had been before, and there appeared to have been a great deal of attention bestowed on her; her cheeks, nose, and upper lip, were rubbed over with red ochre, on which, and under the eyes, were laid spots of white clay; the small of her back was likewise rubbed with ochre, and by her deportment seemed desirous of shewing that she was finer than common. Shortly after two of the convicts being fishing, Banalong finding they had no arms in the boat, went alongside in his canoe, and robbed them of the fish they had taken; his wife and sister being in the canoe, and having several spears, the convicts were deterred from making any resistance. In consequence of this robbery, orders were given that no boat in future should go out of the cove unarmed.

The next day the natives came to the settlement, they were told, that if any more spears were thrown they would all be killed; but these threats did not seem to make the smallest impression on them. Banalong coming soon after, he was charged with taking the fish from the two white men; he denied the charge with great assurance, asserting that he was a great distance from the place at the time; but when the people were confronted with him, he endeavoured to justify himself, but with so insolent an air, that he rather aggravated than excused the offence: he frequently mentioned the man who had been wounded, and threatened revenge; but on recollecting himself, he offered his hand to the governor, which being refused, he grew violent, and seemed inclined to make use of his stick: a centinel was called in, as it was feared he might commit some extravagance that would oblige his excellency to order him to be put to death; for his behaviour was savage and insolent in the extreme, and would have met with instant punishment in any other person; but they wished to bring him to reason, without having recourse to violent measures; and the governor was very unwilling to destroy that confidence he had been at so much pains to create in Banalong, which the slightest punishment would have done: he was therefore desired to come near the governor, but he refused, turned upon his heel, and went away. As he passed the wheelwright's shop, the workmen being at dinner, he stole a hatchet, with which he got clear off.

Chapter XIII.

The natives continued to visit Sydney after Banalong's recent behaviour, and conducted themselves in such a manner as gave great reason to suppose he would never return: this, however, was not the case; for having previously visited the fishing-boats, to know if Governor Philip was still angry with him, and if he would shoot him; he appeared very desirous of knowing if he might go to the governor's house, at the same time naming a man who had stole the hatchet, and denied having used any threats; however not being pleased with the answers that were given to his questions, he went away, but returned in a few days, and went to the governor's, who, happening to see him come to the gate, ordered him away. He was seen soon afterwards, and seemed very desirous of being received again into favour; he disclaimed any knowledge of the hatchet, or any intention of revenging the death of a man who had been shot. Governor Philip appeared to believe him, and he was suffered to go into the yard, which was always open to the natives; some bread and fish were given him, but he was not permitted to enter the house as usual: though this degradation did not a little hurt his pride, he frequently repeated his visits.

Governor Philip had been very desirous of learning the reason that the females had two of the joints of the little finger cut off, and of seeing in what manner that operation was performed; he had now an opportunity of gratifying a part of his wish: Coalby's wife coming to the settlement with a new born female, brought her infant to the governor's house; and being told that his excellency would be present at the operation, it was accordingly performed. A ligature was applied round the little finger at the second joint; but two days afterwards they brought the child again, the ligature was either broken or taken off; this being told the mother, she took some hairs from the head of an officer who was present and bound them very tight round the finger; after some time a gangrene took place; and though the child seemed uneasy when it was touched, it did not cry, nor was any attention paid to it after the ligature was applied. This operation had always been performed on the left hand, but this child was an exception, for it was the little finger of the right hand which underwent the operation: this bandage was continued until the finger was ready to drop off, when its parents took it to the surgeon, who, at their request, separated it with a knife.

Banalong after an absence of three weeks, during which time he had been particularly active in rendering services to a boat's crew, several of whom would have been lost but for his exertions, which were considered as a full atonement for his past behaviour, and he was admitted again into the favour of the governor. In consequence of this reconciliation the number of visitors increased, and the governor's yard became their head quarters.

Their medical operations partake more of the juggling than the Esculapian system. Coalby had formerly been wounded with a fish-gig below the left breast, and though it must have been done many years, as it was extremely difficult to perceive the scar; yet it was supposed that he felt some pain from the straps of a knapsack, which he carried when out on an excursion with the governor: he had travelled two or three days with it on his shoulders, and the straps pressing against his breast he complained of pain there.

He applied to an old man and his son, who had joined them in the excursion, for relief, and they prepared to perform the cure: the son began the ceremony, by taking a mouthful of water, which he spirted on the part affected, and then applying his mouth, began to suck as long as he could without taking breath, which appeared to make him sick, and when he rose up, for his patient was extended at full length on the grass, he walked about for some minutes; he then repeated the function three times, and he appeared, by drawing in his stomach, to feel the same pain he pretended to extract from the breast of his patient; and having picked up a bit of stick or stone, but with so little sleight of hand that it was obvious to the whole party, he pretended to throw something which he had taken out of his mouth into the water. He undoubtedly threw something away, which must have been what he picked up; but Coalby, after the ceremony was over, said it was what he had sucked out of his breast; which was understood to be two barbs of a fish-gig, as he made use of the word bullerdooul; but the governor was of a different opinion, and thought he meant two pains. Before this business was finished, the doctor felt the patient's back below the shoulder, and seemed to apply his fingers, as if he twitched something out: after which he sat down by the patient, and put his right arm round his back; the old man, at the same time, sat down on the other side of the patient, with his face the contrary way, and clasped him round the breast with his right arm; each of them held one of the patient's hands, they continued in this situation several minutes, straining him very close, and thus ended the ceremony, when Coalby said he was perfectly well. He gave his worsted night-cap, and a share of his supper, as a fee to his doctors; and being asked if they were both of the faculty, he said yes, and a little boy that was with them was a doctor too; from whence it was supposed that the power of healing is hereditary, and descended from father to son.

As the natives frequently caught more fish than they could immediately use, great pains had been taken to induce them to barter it with the settlers at Paramatta for bread, vegetables, &c. Several of them had carried on this traffic, and there was reason to hope that a tolerable fish--market would soon be established: among those who brought their fish was a young man that had lived some months with the governor, but had left the settlement from time to time, to go a fishing: his canoe was a new one, and being the first he had ever been master of, he was not a little proud of it, and accordingly valued it highly.

Strict orders had been given that their canoes should never be touched; and indeed the interest of the marines and convicts should have secured them from insult; the traffic and intercourse tending much to their comforts, the balance being greatly in their favour; but in a very short time this amity and good understanding was interrupted by some villains, who had stove the canoe of the young man before-mentioned. The moment he discovered the injury done him, he flew to the governor's in a violent rage, said the white men had broke his canoe, and that he would kill them; he had his throwing-stick, and several spears in his hand, and his hair, face, arms, and his breast were painted red, which is a sign of the most implacable anger. It was not till the governor assured him that he would kill those who had destroyed his canoe, that he would listen to any thing tending to divert him from his purpose of killing the white men; he promised at last that he would leave it to the governor to punish them.

The offenders were soon discovered, and were severely flogged in the presence of Balderry; but he was far from being satisfied, till he was told that one of them had been hanged. During their examination he appeared very impatient, and said that it belonged to him to punish the injury he had received. About a month after, when it was thought he had been amply compensated by various presents which the governor had given him; by seeing the offenders punished; and by supposing one of them had been hanged, yet he took the first opportunity of revenging himself, which plainly shews that these people do not readily forgive an injury. A convict who had strayed from the settlement, was met by two of the natives; and had scarce passed them when he was wounded in the back with a spear, and before he could recover himself he received a second wound in the side; however, he got away; and as they did not attempt to stop him to get cloaths, or take any thing from him, there was no doubt but the destruction of the canoe was the cause of this attack; especially, as the same evening several natives were seen round a fire, and being asked who it was that had wounded the white man, they immediately answered, "Balderry." It is not a little remarkable that these people always tell the names of those who have thrown spears at the colonists, or who have stole any thing from the settlement, if they are asked, though they are conscious you mean to punish them: it might be thought to proceed from a principle of adhering to truth, did they not destroy this opinion by invariably denying any thing they may be charged with, though you see them commit the offence and lay the blame on another who is not present; it is not only surprizing that they always discover the offenders, but this they do openly, without any fear or dread of the consequence.

The destruction of this canoe was a most unfortunate accident, as it prevented the natives from carrying their fish to Paramatta; and no canoe visited the settlement for some time after; and, besides the governor wished to attach Balderry to himself, intending to take him to England when he returned. Balderry began to make enquiries of the various parties he met, whether beanah, the governor, was still angry; he was answered in the affirmative, and told that he would be killed for wounding a white man; yet this did not deter him from coming into the cove in a canoe, and the governor on being made acquainted with his appearance, ordered a party of marines to go and secure him. Banalong, who was present, seeing the soldiers go towards the point, gave him the alarm, and he got off. Governor Philip saw Banalong speaking to the young man in his canoe, and gave him to understand that Balderry should be killed; upon which he called out that the governor was still very angry: on hearing this Balderry paddled off pretty briskly to the opposite side of the harbour, and appeared to set their threats at defiance, and talked of spearing; but whether it was she governor or the soldiers that he threatened could not be distinguished, he being at too great a distance to hear distinctly. These people are very resolute, and when provoked set little value on their lives, so they can be revenged; they ever contrive to be even with you, whether you praise or threathen, and whenever a blow is given they are sure to return it, though their lives should pay for it. A number of natives having arrived at Sydney, amongst whom there were upwards of thirty women and children, they were treated with bread and rice as usual: they informed his excellency that Balderry was on the opposite side of the cove, with a party of his friends, armed. Whether his coming after what had passed proceeded from a supposition that he should not be punished, or that he was safe whilst surrounded by so many of his countrymen, it was thought necessary to order him to be taken, as soon as the visitants should be gone; for as Balderry could not be seized without their hearing the dispute, it was probable they would suppose themselves in danger, and make use of their spears in defence of their countryman, in which case many of them must have been killed; and this was the more likely, as many of the guests were strangers, and this was the first visit to the colony.

As soon as they had taken their leave, a party of soldiers were ordered after the delinquent, but before they got sight of him, he had been advertised of his danger by Nanbarre, who hearing what was going forward, had left the place; a serjeant and a party were sent after him: in their way they met several of the natives, who joined them in a friendly manner, but while they were talking to the serjeant, one of them had the audacity to attempt to wrest a firelock from one of the soldiers; however, he failed in the attempt, but immediately after a spear was thrown, supposed to be by Balderry: two muskets were now fired among the natives, which wounded one of them in the leg, but, unfortunately, neither of the offenders. A strong party was immediately ordered to some brick fields, where a pretty numerous body of them had assembled; but Nanbarre, ever faithful to his countrymen, on seeing the soldiers form on the parade, took to the woods, and stripping himself, that he might not be known, joined the natives, and put them on their guard; after which he returned, and saw the governor pass with some officers whilst he was hid in a bush; he afterwards met an officer's servant, and asked where the governor and soldiers were going; on being told, he laughed, and said they were too late for the people were all gone.

Banalong came in soon afterwards with his wife, and though he was told the soldiers were gone out to take Balderry, yet the intelligence did not prevent him from eating a hearty dinner, and when he went away, he left a large bundle of spears, fish-gigs, and various other articles, under the care of the governor. As the natives knew that the governor only meant to punish those who threw the spears, the late disagreements did not in the least interrupt their visits, and they called upon their friends with the same familiarity as if nothing had happened. They were asked what became of the wounded man; they said he was gone to his tribe; that the wound was but of little consequence, and soon would be healed.

Barangaroo was now near her time of lying-in, when the colonists had an opportunity of seeing their preparations on the occasion: she had two nets hanging from her neck, one of which being new, the governor was desirous of obtaining, and it was given him, after she had taken a large piece of the tea tree out of it, nicely folded up, and which was intended to lay her infant upon, and which is the only preparation previous to the ceremony of an infant's introduction into the world, that is made by lying in women in this country. The bark of the tea tree is thick in proportion to the size of the trunk, and is composed of a great number of layers of very thin bark, not unlike in appearance to the birch tree; but so exquisitely soft, that nothing this country affords can be better calculated for the purpose for which it is intended. Banalong, however, desired to have a blanket for the child, which was given him, and next day a net made in the English manner, which was more acceptable to his wife than the one she had given the governor. Banalong informed the governor that his wife intended to do him the honour of lying-in at his house; this favour his excellency declined, telling him she would be so much better accommodated at the hospital, that he could not think of risking her health, by suffering her to be any where else, which compliment highly gratified both husband and wife, and they accordingly took up their quarters there. Banalong had frequently solicited the governor to receive Balderry again into favour, but was always refused; however, on being told that the poor fellow was extremely ill, the surgeon was desired to go and see him; he found him in a high fever, and the first question he asked, was, whether the governor continued angry with him, and if he would let him go to the hospital to be cured. Banalong, who went with the surgeon, returned to the governor, who told him he was not angry now, and that he might bring his companion to the settlement; he said he would, and early the next morning Balderry made his appearance: at first he was under great apprehensions, but on the governor's taking him by the hand,

and promising that when he was recovered he should live with him again, his fears subsided: he appeared very ill, and went with the surgeon and Banalong to the hospital.

Chapter XIV.

I HAVE been thus minute in detailing the behaviour of the natives, and the persevering diligence and inexhaustible patience of Governor Philip, in conciliating and familiarizing them, in the infancy of the colony, that, should they hereafter attain any degree of civilization, posterity may know to whom they are indebted for the extrication of numberless tribes from the rudest barbarism, thereby adding to society the inhabitants of a country, which occupies a section of the globe of greater extent than all Europe, and capable of becoming a great and powerful empire.

With regard to religion, they sing an hymn, or song of joy, from day--break till sun-rise; but we have not been yet able to discover whether they have any particular object to whom they pay adoration; neither do any of the celestial bodies seem to occupy more of their attention than any of the animals which inhabit this extensive country; yet they do not appear entirely ignorant of a future state, as they say the bones of the dead are in the grave, and their bodies in the clouds; or may probably have been misunderstood, and mean that the soul is in the clouds. They most certainly burn their dead; for on opening a new made grave, a quantity of white ashes were found, which appeared to have been but lately deposited there; among the ashes were found part of a human jaw--bone, and a piece of a skull, which had not been sufficiently burnt to prevent its being perfectly ascertained. The grave was not a foot deep, but the earth was raised as high round it as are the common graves in England. The sun, moon, and stars; they call wera (bad). Araboe once went into fits on seeing a falling star, and said that every body would be destroyed; although some who were present insisted that she particularly alluded to the "murray nowey," the Sirius, which was lost some time after at Norfolk Island. From Banalong we understood they believe in apparitions, which they call "mane;" he describes them as ascending from the earth with a horrid noise, seizing any one in its way by the throat: he says these apparitions singe the hair and beards of those to whom they appear, which he said was a very painful operation; rubbing the face after every application of the firebrand.

Their principal diversion is that of dancing, for which ceremony they prepare themselves with more than ordinary attention; they are all in their birth-day suits, like so many Adams and Eves, without even a fig leaf to parry the inquisitive glance of the curious European. The young women employ all their art in decorating the young men, who are chiefly ornamented with streaks of white, drawn with pipe-clay, and in different forms, according to the taste of the man himself or to the lady who adorns him. They are as emulous of appearing fine as the most finished petit maitre, preparing for the birth-day ball of his favourite mistress. Their paint cannot be applied without moistening; and the lady, in drawing the streaks down the face, which is the most essential part of the decoration, spits in the face of her friend whom she is adorning, from time to time, as the ochre or clay get dry. Their dances are always at the close of the day, as they prefer fire-light to that of the sun on these occasions.

The dance begins by a few young boys, and is encreased by the men and women gradually falling in, to the number of thirty or forty, but mostly men; it is truly wild and savage, yet in many parts order and regularity are very apparent. One man would frequently single himself out from the rest, and running round the whole of the performers, sing out in a loud voice, some expression delivered in a peculiar tone of voice; he would then fall in with the rest of the dancers, who alternately led forward in the centre, and there exhibit their utmost skill and dexterity in the most difficult contortions of the body, which, in their opinion, constitute principal beauties of dancing: one of the most striking is that of placing their feet very wide apart, and by an extraordinary exertion of the muscles of the thighs and legs, move their knees in a trembling and very astonishing manner, such as no person in the colony could any ways imitate; of course much practice is required to arrive at any degree of perfection in this singular motion. There is great variety in their dances; sometimes they dance in pairs, and frequently turn back to back, then suddenly turn and face each other; sometimes they all sit on the ground, with their feet under them, in the manner of the Chinese, and at a particular word or signal they are on their feet in a moment, which they perform without any assistance from their hands; they then run back in rows, and again advance in the same order, Sometimes they form a circle with some distinguished person in the centre; at other times all the dancers have green boughs in their hands: in all the different figures they generally finish by a certain number of their principal dancers advancing to the front, and go through the difficult part of the dance, the quivering motion of the knees, upon which the whole company faces to the front, and go through the same motions, the most expert being generally in the centre. Their music consists of two sticks of very hard wood, one of which the musician holds to his breast, in the manner of a violin, and strikes it with the other, in tolerable good time. The performer sing the whole time of the dance; assisted by several boys and girls who are seated at his feet, and by the manner of crossing their thighs form a hollow between them and their belly, upon which they beat time with the flat of the hand, which makes an odd tho not disagreeable sound. They are very prone to flattery and if any strangers are present, always ask for their approbation, and appear highly delighted if you say "boojerie eariberie," a very good dance--which never fails to produce more than extraordinary exertions.

They are very desterous in striking fish: the spear of the gig with which they take them is about ten feet In length, but they can increase it by joints, as we do our fishing-rods in England; they have several prongs barbed with the bone of a fish, or of some animal.

The fisher lies across the canoe, his face in the water, and his fish-gig, ready for darting; thus he lies motionless, and by his face being beneath the surface, he can see the fish distinctly; in this manner they strike the fish with great certainty. The women are chiefly employed with lines and hooks; the lines manufactured from the bark of trees, the hooks commonly of the pearl of different shells: the talons of birds of prey they sometimes make use of, but the former are most esteemed. The women are frequently seen is a miserable canoe with two or three children, fishing the whole day in the edge of a surf that would terrify an old seaman to trust himself near in a good stout boat. The men are excellent divers, and remain a surprizing time in the surfs where their canoes cannot live: whatever they bring up to the surface they throw on shore, where their comrade attends to receive it. Having a fire ready kindled for cooking, they broil or roast all their food; they have not the least conception of boiling, for one of the natives watching an opportunity when nobody was attending to the kettle, plunged his hand into the boiling water to take the fish: of course, to his utter astonishment, he was terribly scalded. They procure fire with great labour, by fixing the pointed end of a round stick into a hole made in a flat piece of wood, and whirling it round swiftly with both hands, sliding them up and down till the operator is fatigued, when he is relieved by some of his companions; each takes his turn till the fire is produced: from the labour attending this process, it is no wonder that they are seldom seen without a piece of lighted wood in their hand. When they mean to evince a partiality to any stranger, they immediately assume his name, calling him by theirs; this they consider as the highest compliment they can pay an English-man, and are highly pleased at being called by their new name. Of all their customs, that of making love would be the farthest from meeting the approbation of my fair countrywomen, that ceremony being in this country always prefaced by a sound beating, which the lady receives as a matter of course, with all the meekness imaginable.

Chapter XV.

WE had now upwards of a thousand acres of cleared land at Paramatta, three hundred and fifty of which were in wheat and maize; but though we had frequent showers of rain, yet not in sufficient quantities to compensate for the excessive drought which had been experienced in the preceding months; and from the ground being new, and requiring more work than was in the power of the settlers to bestow on it, the grain in general had a very unpromising appearance. There are about two hundred acres laid out in gardens, as much more prepared for turnips and potatoes, and the remainder closed in for feeding cattle. We are very badly off for manure, and ere the colony can properly flourish it must be stocked with cattle, the ground being infinitely too poor of itself ever to produce crops sufficient for us to depend on it solely for subsistence. The sudden vicissitudes of the weather must also render our harvests very precarious, as well as prove injurious to the health of the new comers; it often happens that there is a change of from forty to fifty degrees twice in one day. It is no unfrequent circumstance to see the country strewed with numbers of birds, fallen from the trees, unable to support the intense heat of the meridian sun. Numbers of convicts fall victims, but it must not be wholly ascribed to the weather, as the debilitated state in which they are for the most part landed, would, were it a more favourable climate, be attended with a considerable mortality; and they are generally so weak that they cannot be put to any kind of labour, but are employed in weeding and pulling grass for the purpose of thatching: we have frequently four or five hundred on the doctor's list, who are individually visited daily by the surgeon; upwards of fifty have died in a month, in the generality of whom nature appears entirely exhausted, and many of them were so fairly worn out, that they expired without a groan, and, to all appearance, did not experience the smallest degree of pain.

From a most humane suggestion of Captain Parker, of the Gorgon, the governor issued orders for a regular survey to be taken of the condition of the convicts on their landing from the different transports; and a strict investigation taking place, it appeared that some of the captains had very much abridged their unfortunate passengers of the allowance stipulated by government for their subsistence; and this inhuman practice had been carried to such an extent in some of the ships, that it appeared many had been literally starved to death. A strong and pointed representation of the circumstance was sent home to government, which will, I hope, put an effectual stop to such nefarious proceedings.

Some of the convicts had entertained an idea that they could range along the coast till they reached some of the Chinese settlements; subsisting themselves on oysters and other shell-fish, having been told that there was a copper, coloured tribe one hundred and fifty miles to the northward, who were much more civilized than the natives they were with, and who traficked with the Dutch from Timor, where they would be free. With these notions several parties set off from Sydney Cove and Rose Hill, but after some days straggling some were taken, and others returned of their own accord, induced by the imperative command of hunger; and as some were supposed to be still lurking in the woods, afraid of returning, lest they should be punished for leaving the settlement, the governor less inclined to punish than to convince them of their error, promised a general pardon to every one who should return within five days; at the same time declaring that an exemplary punishment would be inflicted on those who should be taken after that period. Accordingly several returned, and appeared sensible of the lenity shewn them, but some of them appeared capable of the most desperate attempts, and even talked of repelling force by force; they were, however, given to understand that no mercy would be shewn them on the least disposition to mutiny, and that any who were near those that might be so disposed would be considered as principals, and treated accordingly. Almost all the deserters returned, and those who were still missing, was supposed to be murdered by the natives, and the miserable state of those that returned would, it was thought, most effectually prevent any more excursions of the like nature.

The purchases I had made at the Cape, as well as the presents I brought from England, enabled me to furnish the officers and settlers with various little articles, which in general were not to be had by the ships, so that in a short time I had collected the following valuable stock for my farm yard; a sow in pig; two fine porkers; a young she goat and two kids; an English dunghill cock, three laying hens, and one with a brood of chickens and young ducks: these, with a young kangaroo, which I had been at infinite pains in rearing, three native dogs, myself, a convict woman servant, and her son Timothy, a youth between twelve and thirteen, a tractable and useful lad, comprised the whole family. Having always had a strong predilection for horticulture, the garden employed great part of my time, and is now as prosperous and flourishing as any in the colony. Governor Philip, when he visits Rose Hill, takes a great delight in it, and gives me much credit for its improvement, as well as for the appearance and spirit of industry manifest in the convicts under my superintendance.

Having contracted an intimacy with a young man, who had taken one of the farms on the northern boundary, about four miles from Paramatta, I generally walked over once or twice a week: as I was returning from thence one afternoon, with no other company but my boy Tim, who, having evinced a great partiality for me, was now my constant companion, a large male kangaroo crossed the path just before us: I immediately took my gun from the boy, fired at the animal, and disabled one of his hind legs, which very much impeded his flight; however, he preserved his distance for near an hour, when getting a fair shot at him, I lodged a ball in the back part of his head, which effectually did his business.

Upon examining our prize, I found it would be impossible for us to get it home without help: we therefore searched for a place to conceal it till the next afternoon, when I meant to return for it with a couple of men: a few paces from where it lay we perceived a cavity on the slope of a deep ravine, to which we dragged the carcase, and covering it with stones and grass, began to think of making the best of our way to the settlement.

The sun was now setting, and I began to be alarmed at being so far from home: in the eagerness of our pursuit I had forgot to take any bearings by my pocket compass, and the day closing ere we had reached any known path, increased my apprehensions in the extreme. Poor Tim, though half dead with fatigue, endeavoured to keep up my spirits, which he perceived were much agitated: "He was certain sure," he said, "that we were in the right road, and that we should get home time enough to muster the people at nine, the hour fixed for that purpose; and that if we were obliged to sleep in the woods, why, he would cut some grass for my bed, and stand centinel with the gun while I lay down, for he was not afraid to fire: and besides, my dear master," added he, "you know the natives are so 'feard of guns, that should they come I only need show it, and they'll be off like a shot." The boy's courage and fidelity charmed me, and put me to the blush to think I had so little command of myself as not to conceal my uneasiness from him.

After rambling for near two hours, we could not perceive that we were any nearer home than at sunset, but rather conjectured we had taken a different rout, as we did not recollect a single object that now presented itself; it being a fine star-light night, we could distinguish the river at times through the trees at some distance; but presenting a different appearance to any part we had ever seen; we quickened our pace with the hope of speedily reaching its banks, when to my great mortification, we were stopped by a deep ravine. I now abandoned all hopes of reaching the settlement; and, as the poor boy was almost exhausted with fatigue, made up my mind to pass the night on the spot.

With this determination we began to cut grass, and pull some boughs, in order to make a fire; for although it had been intensely hot in the middle of the day, I could now very well have dispensed with a great coat. While I was thus employed, Tim, who had got some distance from me, came running back, saying I might save myself the trouble, for he had found a snug sleeping place for us, with plenty of dried wood for a fire. I followed him to the spot, and found it was a hut inhabited by the natives when hunting; as I had no apprehensions of their returning, the hunting season having just closed, I got a light from a flash of powder, and in a few minutes kindled a comfortable fire. In one corner of the hut was a bundle of grass ready dried, which we spread to lie down on; but I could not prevail on the boy to think of sleep; no, if I would trust him with the gun he would keep watch. Not being inclined to sleep myself, I took a book from my pocket, and, by fire-light, endeavoured to amuse myself till day-break, I had scarce perused half a dozen pages, ere poor Tim had sunk into a sound sleep; how long it was before I followed his example, or how long I should have continued it, is difficult to determine, had I not been waked by an acute pain in one of my hands, which I found was occasioned by the bite of some ants, whom I had accidentally molested in my sleep: I called Tim, and sallied forth; following the winding of the ravine about a mile, we arrived at its termination, and perceived a break in high lands before us, through which I distinctly saw Rose Hill, about six or seven miles distant; this prospect revived our spirits, which were beginning to flag, with the reflection that if we escaped every other danger, that of being starved to death was inevitable, unless we could extricate ourselves from the labyrinth in which we were involved. Having set the spot by my compass, I found it bore W. S. W. as we descended to the plain we lost sight of the object, but continued our course in that direction till we arrived at a swamp, which cost us some time in getting round, there being no possibility of crossing it: we had now got to a part almost impassable, from the quantity of underwood, and the trees were so close together, that we could scarce see three yards before us, and were proceeding very slowly through a thicket, when we were alarmed by a deep groan, apparently but a few paces distant; a sound so unlooked for, for some time rivetted us to the spot. Not being immediately able to perceive from whence the groan issued, I advanced with great caution about a dozen paces, when I discovered a cave in the side of a rock; I was at first for retreating, but on recollecting that perhaps I might render some service to the afflicted, and that I equally stood in need of assistance, or perhaps might perish with hunger; I examined the priming of my gun, forced Tim, with some difficulty behind me, and approaching the entrance of the cave, a most interesting scene presented itself to my view: a young creature seated on a jut of the rock, mournfully contemplating the extended body of a man, whose expiring groans had just pierced our cars; all her faculties were so absorbed with grief, that we were yet unnoticed: a sympathising sorrow pervaded all my frame; I gave my gun to Tim, and made signs for him to retire, lest the sight should alarm her; when she perceived me she uttered a faint shriek, and sunk motionless on the body. Observing a small pond a few paces from the cave, I sent the boy to bring some water in his hat, and gently moved her from the body to the mouth of the cave, raised her up, and supported her in my arms; the water soon brought her too, when she raised her head, and regarded me with a look blended with grief and terror; I endeavoured, by every sign I could suggest, to do away her fears, and retired a few paces, leaving her at liberty to go from the cave had she chose. Gaining confidence by my behaviour, she made me understand that the deceased was her brother, who, faint with the loss of blood, could not reach their habitation, and night approaching, they had turned from the road to shelter themselves in this cave. On examining the body I found a deep wound under the left pap, made with a spear, part of which, being barbed, remained in the wound: I made her understand, partly by signs, and partly by some words I had picked up, that I had unfortunately lost my way, and had been all night in the woods: she shook her head, and pointed to her brother, signifying that she could not leave him, but that their habitation was not far off, and making me observe a hill about two miles distant, gave me to understand it was in their neighbourhood. I made signs to her, that if she would go and acquaint her friends with her situation, I would watch by her brother till her return: her eye glistened with joy as she gathered my meaning, and with an assenting inclination of the head, more eloquent and expressive of her feelings than in the power of the most refined language to convey, she quitted us with a celerity, quickened by fraternal love, and in a few moments was out of sight.

This interesting and pathetic scene had so wholly absorbed all my faculties, that not a single reflection of danger had occurred to me in the approaching interview, when Tim, who had been witness to several instances of the perfidy of the natives towards the settlers, strongly urged me to leave the body, and make the best of our way home. Roused by his solicitations, a momentary impulse of fear came over me, and my mind had half yielded to his importunity, when casting my eyes on the body methought I perceived it heave; a feeble sigh convinced me that life was yet unextinguished, and the imperative call of humanity decided my operations: a deathlike dew had bespread his face and limbs, which I dried with my handkerchief, and chafed his body with my hand. Tim most readily bore his part in this act of humanity, and a returning warmth encouraged us to redouble our efforts; in a few moments we peceived a faint pulsation, which gradually increased: at this juncture we were surprised by the return of his sister, accompanied by her father, another elderly man, and a boy about twelve years of age: seeing us busy about the body, they stopped short at the entrance of the hut, seemingly at a loss for our conduct.

I beckoned my young friend, who advanced with the utmost confidence, and giving her the hand of her brother, she exclaimed, with great emotion, "Didgery-goor, didgery-goor," I thank you, I thank you;--and turning to her father, called him to her: I immediately quitted my station, and resigned him to their care; the old man examined the wound, and with great seeming skill examined the barb; during the operation the youth lifted up his eyes, and observing his father, a glance of filial affection beamed forth. Hope now tranquilised the boding fears of the little group; Yeariana, his sister, supported him while the father and his friends were contriving how they should remove him to their dwelling; finding it necessary to dispatch some one for their canoe, the river which passed their habitation winding within fifty paces of us, and which was the safest and only conveyance he could bear; Yeariana proposed going for it; and it being our direct road to Paramatta, I seized the opportunity of accompanying her; in less than an hour we arrived at the foot of a small mountain, when Yeariana, like an arrow from a bow, abruptly quitted us, leaving her brother, the boy before mentioned, as our guide. We were not long before we discovered near a dozen natives, with Yeariana at their head, waiting our arrival; she had sent off the canoe for her brother, and had got some dried fish, which she presented us, and led us to her hut or cave, which was a large excavated rock on the bank of a very pleasant branch of the river. The reception we met with from this grateful people almost bordered upon adoration; the mother of Yeariana was quite troublesome with her caresses for my service to her son; and I could perceive in the mild eye of her daughter that it anxiously sought a farther acquaintance. Upon enquiry I found we were near five miles from Paramatta, but that none of them had ever visited the settlement; however, Batcherry, her brother, offered to be our conductor, provided I would take care of him, and see him part of the way next day; promising to see her again shortly, I took my leave, and arrived at Paramatta about noon, heartily fatigued. My absence had not caused any alarm at the settlement, as they thought I had gone to Sydney Cove, which I had done twice or thrice, and staid there all night.

Every object that presented itself to Batcherry, filled him with surprise and astonishment, and the poor lad had scarce time to eat or drink, so much was he taken up with admiration of the wonders that surrounded him. The next morning I set him on his way home, giving him a hatchet for himself, and a string of beads for his sister, whose image had made a strong impression on my mind, being the most interesting I ever saw; with a form that might serve as a perfect model for the most scrupulous statuary; her face and hair unlike any thing I had ever seen in this country; the first of a perfect oval, or Grecian shape, with features regularly beautiful, and as fine a pair of eyes as can be imagined; the latter long, and of a shining black; she was likewise of a much lighter colour than any of her countrywomen, and might easily have been taken for a beautiful Oriental Creole.

Taking three men, and the boy Tim, we went in search of the spot where we had concealed the kangaroo, and with some difficulty found it; we cut a couple of stout sticks, and laying the animal across it, took spell and spell till we reached home, when I rewarded the men with a fore quarter for their trouble.

It was more than a week ere I could spare time to pay a visit to the abode of my charming Yeariana; when arranging my business so that, should I be detained all night, my absence would be no material consequence, I took Tim with me, and with much more facility than I expected, found my way to Paculbenah, the name of the place where the family of Yeariana resided; Batcherry saw us as we turned the foot of the mountain, and running back to the cave, gave notice of our coming: the whole family, except Palerino, who was not sufficiently recovered, were ranged at the entrance of their cave; their joy at seeing me was evident in their countenances; the old man took me by the hand, and led me to his son, who was now out of danger; he expressed his thanks by a hearty squeeze of the hand, and a look that amply explained his meaning; his sister was not deficient in expressions of satisfaction, by every little attention in her power. Having brought plenty of beef, bread, and a little brandy with us, lest we might stand in need of refreshment, we seated ourselves in a circle on the ground, and spread our fare on a piece of canvass which had contained it; every eye was fixed on me, and every motion gave fresh cause of wonder. There being no knives among them, I carved the meat for them all, and gave to every one a part; the beef they eat with great avidity, but did not relish the bread, and rinsed their mouths several times after it. When the meat was all eaten, they produced some dried fish, roots, and two or three kinds of berries, and a nut resembling the chesnut in taste: every person having finished eating, Wanjarkoo, the father, clapping his hands thrice, they all started upon their feet, and prepared to resume their usual avocations; the old man and his wife went to the canoe to finish their day's fishing; Batcherry to cut grass; and Yeariana was left to attend her brother. Palerino, who lay on a bed of dried grass in one corner of the hut; she, after some minutes pause, took my hand, and drawing me towards Palerino, joined it with his, and whispering something to him, he cried "Boojerie, boojerie," Good, good Pelerino--and by signs asked my name, when I repeated "George," two or three times; then squeezing my hand to his breast, he made me understand that he would change names with me, and I must call him George, and he call me Palerino, and that he would come and bring Yeariana with him to the settlement, as soon as he was well: this ceremony was finished by his sister kissing us both, repeating "Boojerie Palerino, boojerie George," Good Palerino, good George, and appeared quite over-joyed. They now made me understand, that the day before I found them, as they had been out together, searching for a kind of grub, which is a part of their food, they were surprized by two of the tribe of Wangal, their mortal enemies, one of whom her brother had killed with a fish gig; during the conflict she had thrown a stone at the surviver, which so disabled him, that he retreated with difficulty to his canoe, and rowed off with precipitation. Palerino faint with the loss of blood, could not reach their habitation, and night approaching, they had turned from the road to shelter themselves in the cave where I found them.

Highly pleased with my visit, I took leave an hour before sunset, when they repeated their assurances of coming to the settlement, which was what I ardently wished for, as I flattered myself I should be able to persuade them to stay some time with us, and thereby cement that friendship which had just taken root, and might eventually prove beneficial to the settlement, as well as promote certain views just dawning on my mind with respect to Yeariana.

Mr. Wentworth, who resides at Norfolk Island, had been appointed to the same station there that I occupy at Paramatta, which joined to his skill in surgery, renders him an invaluable acquisition; and as we frequently correspond, he has kindly promised me an account of the rise and progress of that settlement: he speaks with rapture of the urbanity of Governor King to all ranks and descriptions, and whose unremitting attention to the clearing and cultivating the land, already enables the settlers, of which there are between forty and fifty sailors and marines, who have parcels of land allotted them of sixty acres each, and about twenty convicts who have ten acres each, not only to support themselves, but to have something to spare; indeed, they have greatly the advantage of those settled at Sydney and Paramatta, the ground being much more fertile; the wheat frequently producing an increase of twenty fold, and it is conjectured that future harvests will be more productive. Potatoes thrive exceedingly, upwards of a hundred having been seen to a single root, and every kind of garden vegetable shoots up in abundance, and in the greatest perfection.

To ascertain in what time a man might be able to cultivate ground sufficient to support himself, the governor about a twelvemonth ago, ordered an acre of ground to be cleared in a good situation; it was then given to a very decent, steady convict, who was told, that if he was industrious, in order to prove the experiment, he should have thirty acres given him, cleared in like manner. He was very assiduous, and at the expiration of six months, requested another acre to be cleared for him, which was granted; and he is now able to support himself, without drawing any assistance from the public stores.

The declining health of our worthy governor rendering his return to England indispensible for its re-establishment, he made the necessary arrangements for the future government of the colony: and having persuaded Banalong and another native to accompany him, embarked on board the Atlantic transport, and with the benedictions of every person in the settlement, proceeded on his voyage to England.

THE END

CPSIA information can be obtained
at www.ICGtesting.com
Printed in the USA
LVOW10s1204070518
576274LV00006B/1155/P

9 781494 406486